THE NEW COMPLETE
SHETLAND
SHEEPDOG

Minos Amadeus and Ch. Minos The Escape Artist, a photogenic duo, owned by Chris Gabrielides.

THE NEW COMPLETE
SHETLAND
SHEEPDOG

Maxwell Riddle

HOWELL
BOOK HOUSE
New York

Howell Book House
Macmillan General Reference
A Simon & Schuster Macmillan Company
15 Columbus Circle
New York, NY 10023

Library of Congress Cataloging-in-Publication Data

Riddle, Maxwell.
　　The new complete Shetland sheepdog / Maxwell Riddle.
　　　　p.　cm.
　　Rev. ed. of : The new Shetland sheepdog. 1st ed. 1974.
　　ISBN 0-87605-333-9
　　1. Shetland sheepdog.　I. Riddle, Maxwell.　New Shetland sheepdog.
II. Title.
SF429.S62R52　1991　　　　　91-20714　CIP
636.7'37—dc20

10 9 8 7 6 5 4 3

Printed in the United States of America

Dedication

THIS BOOK is affectionately dedicated to Elizabeth D. (Betty) Whelen, multitalented breeder, trainer, exhibitor of Shetland Sheepdogs and at times Collies and Afghan Hounds; active member of the West Country Beagles, and so a rider to hounds after the red fox; photographer, poet and author of that great book *No Greater Love*. I met her first at shows between the great wars, and during and after, when, in company with Eleanor Mann, we would meet at shows, share lunches and talk dogs and shows. And we would plan to meet at the next show. And so I dedicate this book to Betty Whelen, and bow to the memory of Eleanor Mann. And bow again to the recently deceased Margaret Osborne.

Margaret Osborne was a world authority on many breeds of dogs. But her greatest love she gave to the Shetland Sheepdog. She showed her first "from Shiel Sheltie" in 1925. She was already a world authority in the years between the two world wars. She was the only person I ever knew who had been shipwrecked on a desert island. This came during the early part of the Second World War. She was returning from judging in Australia when a German raider attacked the ship and sank it.

Some of those on board managed to reach a desert island. They were rescued a few days later.

In August of 1972 she judged Shelties at the Ravenna Show.

Margaret was eighty when she died, alone except for her faithful Sheltie companion.

The late Elizabeth D. Whelen of the renowned Pocono Shetland Sheepdogs.

Table of Contents

Acknowledgments

T HIS SECOND and greatly expanded edition of *The New Shetland Sheepdog* was made possible by the enthusiastic and unselfish aid of many people. First and foremost are those statistical giants of the breed, Karen Hofstetter, who operates the Sheltie Library at Louisville, Kentucky, and Leslie Rogers, the librarian of Langley, British Columbia.

In Japan, the Japan Kennel Club, the globe-trotting all-breeds judge Kazumassa Igarashi and Junko Kimura helped. Then there were Ferelith Somerfield, editor of *English Dog World*, Ed Croad, New Zealand worldwide all-breeds judge, and from Australia, Lynne Harwood, judge and conservationist. And also the American and Canadian Kennel Clubs and the Cleveland Public Library.

Dr. Sue Ann Bowling, a passionate and highly skilled researcher, has contributed a section on early registration, a study of the lines and families of the great sires, plus an incomparable sire chart. Her study of the blue merles is also incomparable. Barbara Curry's great chapter on grooming is held over, as are Jean D. Simmonds' correct drawings. Barbara Curry and Mary Van Wagenen combined to study the first text to correct errors, both textual and typographical.

Finally, Jill Conard's skillful typing has taken the pressure off my arthritic fingers.

To all, my grateful thanks.

Am., Can. Ch. Cataway's Swiss Aire, CD, HC, owned by Cataway Kennels.

Foreword to the Second Edition

$\mathbf{F}$RIENDS OF THE SHETLAND SHEEPDOG have many reasons to count their blessings. They share their lives with a breed that claims a host of assets: Shelties are small, highly intelligent, trainable, easy to care for, handsome and popular enough to allow for meaningful breeding programs but not so much in demand as to be found in the hands of those who care nothing for the Sheltie's identity and integrity.

Another reason Shetland Sheepdog people have to celebrate is the fact that no less a legend in the dog world than Maxwell Riddle admired the breed so much that he devoted a book to it. When *The New Shetland Sheepdog* first appeared in 1974, it achieved the status of a breed classic almost immediately. This was due, in very large part, to the author's diligence in researching, studying, compiling and using the peerless well of his own dog knowledge and his own memory to make this book what it did, in fact, become. His legendary expedition to the Shetland Islands amply demonstrates his singular dedication to scholarship.

Now comes *The New Complete Shetland Sheepdog*, the first new edition of this great book. Here is the ideal learning tool for more recent fanciers and an accurate chronicle continuing the breed's story from the mid-1970s to the present for those who were there when the first edition came on the scene.

To the best from the original edition come new chapters spotlighting recent winners and leading fanciers, intelligent consideration of matters of concern for every enthusiast and the most reliable guidance for everyone wishing to learn more about the Sheltie for any reason.

Whether you have owned Shetland Sheepdogs for many years, are just starting with your first puppy, are considering acquiring a Sheltie or want more information on history, family lines, genetic inheritance, the breed Standard, obedience participation or a wealth of other aspects, here is where you will find it wonderfully well-documented.

We at Howell Book House are proud of having published this worthy new edition of a truly great book. We are also proud of our long and cordial relationship with its author, one of the finest and most modest gentlemen the dog sport has ever produced.

We wish for you good reading, good learning and continued enjoyment of the Shetland Sheepdogs that brighten your life.

THE PUBLISHER

The author, Maxwell Riddle.   *Robert Seton*

THE NEW COMPLETE
SHETLAND
SHEEPDOG

Ch. Starhaven's Sultra, owned by the Starhaven Kennels of Carl and Amy Langhorst.

Ch. Benayr Here Comes Trouble, ROM, owned by Sharon and Sondra Mauzy and bred by Susan Bentley.

1

Sheepdog Origins

WHAT is a sheepdog? One can answer the question superficially in two sentences. A shepherd is one who tends sheep. And a sheepdog is a shepherd's dog. Some sheepdogs, notably the German Shepherd, are called shepherd dogs. But most shepherds' dogs are called sheepdogs. However, this tells you virtually nothing about a sheepdog. One might paraphrase Gertrude Stein's famous phrase about a rose: A dog is a dog is a dog. But a sheepdog is something more than just the physical being we call a dog. It is a marvelous combination of instincts and aptitudes, conscience, responsibility and intelligence.

To understand how the sheepdog developed—or at least why—you must start at a point long before the beginnings of recorded history. Early humans had been food gatherers and vegetarians. Evidence indicates that, during the Paleolithic Age—the Stone Age—only the dog was domesticated. This may have come 100,000 years ago.

But man became a hunter, a meat eater. During the period that has sometimes been called the Mesolithic Age—the transitional age—domestication of almost all the plants and animals that we have today was accomplished. At last when the Neolithic Age—the New Stone Age—arrived, it began with the triumph of agriculture.

People had discovered that they need no longer hunt for all their food. They could keep domestic animals for food and clothing, and they could grow annual crops. Sheep were the first of the food animals to be domesticated. The time was 8,000 to 10,000 years ago. Cattle and horses came later. Solving some problems for people, they also created other problems.

The sheep of those far-off days must have been far more difficult to handle than are the gentle animals of today. For one thing, they were closer to their wild relatives. For another, they were constantly in danger of death from attacks by wolves, lions and other carnivorous predators. There was an abundance of these in the forests, in mountain lairs, on the plains and on what we would call "grazing land." Even if domestic to a point, the sheep would remember their past. Safety lay in the stampede. Let a few die that the rest might live.

Probably the dogs of the time were both large and ferocious. They were too close to their own wild state not to have been so. We can assume that they had weather-resistant coats, which would be double—an outer coat of guard hairs, and a soft, dense undercoat. Since sheep raising was done in temperate and northerly climates, rather than in the tropics, we can suppose that the dogs were of northern, Spitz-family type. But these qualities do not make a sheepdog. They were—and are—important. More important still is the character of the dog.

Their owners must have noted variances in behavior. They watched and studied their dogs. A dog would act in a certain way. Its owner, with the remarkable understanding he had of animals, would recognize the unconscious act of the dog. It would be useful. So the dog would be trained to perform consciously that act which it had done automatically. Owners would search for other dogs with similar traits. And the best of these would be bred together.

Some dogs fight silently. Others growl, roar and make a terrible noise. The first dog might attack a predator and drive it off without scaring the sheep over which it guarded. But the battle noise of the second dog might frighten the sheep into a stampede.

Perhaps the ancient shepherd noted that some dogs liked to show their dominance by driving the sheep, by making them move this way or that. Such a dog might be trained to herd sheep. The Swiss lake dwellers taught their dogs to drive the sheep into the lake huts at night. The bridge could then be lifted. Such driving dogs would be useful only if they did not get so excited that they attacked the sheep. Those with the necessary restraint would be used for breeding.

These unknown shepherds noted that some dogs seemed to have a natural instinct to guard—a property-guarding instinct, it is called. They noted that dogs, as do wolves, mark out territories for themselves. Such dogs will chase out invading dogs. But then, the shepherds must have noticed that some dogs, having a guarding instinct, also insisted upon keeping the sheep inside the home territory. They bred for this characteristic also. So they developed dogs that seemed to claim ownership of the flock.

Shepherds have always claimed that their dogs could count and seem to know when one of the flock is missing, setting out to round it up. Some dogs appeared to learn by themselves to keep a flock moving toward a water hole or along a trail. All these traits observed by the prehistoric shepherds were bred to and strengthened.

It seems unlikely that these ancient breeders paid any attention to type. In the northern latitudes, a double weather-resistant coat was necessary. This was a natural feature of the northern, Spitz-family dogs. A thick neck ruff was also important, since it protected the throat during battle. Northern dogs also had erect or semierect ears. Dogs with erect ears probably hear better and can locate the direction of sound better and quicker than drop-eared dogs. This trait also would be kept. So would the speed and the ability to stop quickly and to turn sharply.

But type, as we know it today, was probably ignored. Such type as did develop came through other factors. Villages were often isolated. Village dogs were bred to village dogs, and a sort of vague local type did develop. The dogs had a common heritage. An occasional crossbreeding hardly disturbed this. Unless the cross produced some factor that the shepherds considered to be of value, it quickly disappeared from the line.

Even today, if one goes into the farming areas of America, older people are likely to ask: "What has become of the old-fashioned 'farm shepherd dog'?" These were not purebreds. They were bred for performance and not for type. But they belonged to an ancestral type just the same. Vaguely, they resembled the northern dogs. They had prick or semiprick ears, fairly long outer guard coats and soft, dense undercoats. They had a neck ruff and a curving tail with a thick brush. It is not hard to believe that the genes of those dogs still exist in the Shetland Sheepdog.

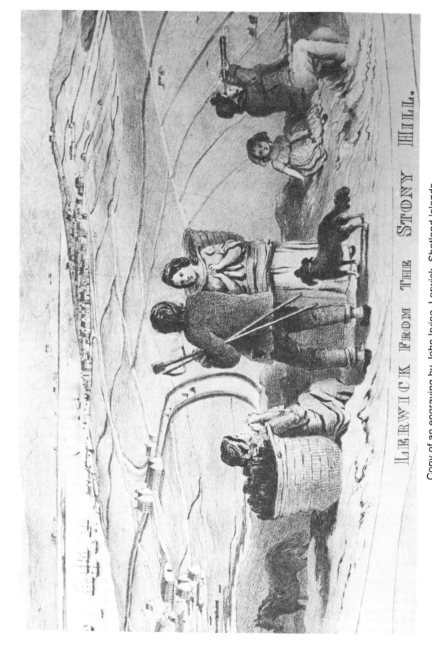

LERWICK FROM THE STONY HILL.

Copy of an engraving by John Irvine, Lerwick, Shetland Islands.

2

The Shetland Islands

THE SHETLAND SHEEPDOG was first developed in the Shetland Islands. It is necessary, therefore, to consider the breed's original home. The Shetland Islands stretch northward from a point about 130 miles north of the northernmost point of the Scottish mainland. There are about one hundred islands large enough to be called islands, and perhaps one hundred more which are not.

The largest island is called Mainland. It is fifty miles long, but is quite narrow. About one third of the way up the island is the village of Lerwick. It is the county seat. Lying on the east side of the island, Lerwick has a good harbor protected by a smaller island, called Bressay.

Aside from Mainland, the major islands are Yell and Unst. Unst is the northernmost, and Muckle Flugga Lighthouse is the northernmost point in the United Kingdom. It was on Unst that the finest scarves were knitted. They were so fine that an island boast is that they can be drawn through an average-size wedding ring.

The islands cover a land area of 549 square miles. Northmaven, on the northern part of Mainland, has Ronas Hill. It is 1,475 feet above sea level and is the highest point on any of the islands. The scenery on most of the islands is ruggedly beautiful. The coast is indented with sea lochs or voes which are often enclosed by steep walls or hills. There are very few trees and in many places the soil is thin and of poor quality.

Only a small part of the islands lie below latitude 60 degrees. That means that they are in roughly the same latitude as Bergen, Norway, or even farther north. Yet the climate is not as cold as might be expected. The reason lies in the

American Gulf Stream. As it breaks away from the American coast, the Gulf Stream breaks up into several branches. Sometimes these are lumped together as the North Atlantic Current. One branch enters the Norwegian Sea to the north of Scotland. Another turns southward into the North Sea.

The current warms the Shetland Islands. But it also helps to set up ceaseless winds. These winds are so strong and so steady that few trees can exist. As at Punta Arenas at the southern tip of South America, vegetable gardens must be sheltered from these winds. Mighty storms rage across the islands. Yet there are pleasant days in the summer, and daylight lasts nearly twenty-four hours. Tennis and golf games are held annually at midnight.

The population of the islands has steadily declined during the last hundred years. Wool growing no longer supplies sufficient income for the remaining islanders, most of whom fish during a part of the year. In recent years, the development of synthetic fabrics has further cut the demand for wool. And modern fishing fleets, which roam the world and use highly sophisticated means for locating fish, have severely cut down fish populations. Refrigeration and world population increases have helped to make commercial fishing a worldwide industry. For these reasons, fishing off the islands has declined as a source of local income. There are, however, quick-freezing and fish meal plants.

The Shetland Islands are sometimes called Zetland. Both names come from the Norwegian, Hjaltland. The Norse have left a heavy influence on the islands. They were, in fact, Norwegian until 1468 when the Shetland and Orkney Islands were pledged for the dowry of Princess Margaret of Norway, who married James III of Scotland. The islands became the property of Scotland.

The wool from the Shetland sheep is very fine. It is also light. The crofters, or their wives and daughters, made loosely woven scarves, gloves, socks and sweaters in patterns known for centuries as "Shetland" or "Fair Isle." But in our time the term has come to mean a fine wool. Today, most fine wool garments titled "Shetland" probably come from mainland Scotland.

A simple way to describe a crofter is to say that he is a tenant farmer. Crofting is an ancient way of life in Scotland and in the Orkney and Shetland Islands. A crofter lives with his family in a small home on the land he rents. He pays an annual rental, cultivates what land is arable and raises sheep, cattle and ponies. In former times, the cattle were light and rather small, but they gave comparatively large amounts of milk. The Shetland pony has spread all over the world. It is not, as sometimes stated, a miniature horse since it differs from the horse in many respects, apart from size. Unlike the horse, it does not require grains. It can live all winter on hay alone, or upon hay and such grasses as it can find. Nor does it require shelter. Those ponies bred in the islands are able to stand both the raging storms and the ceaseless winds.

Wolves and other carnivorous predators disappeared from the islands centuries ago. But sheepdogs were needed. They could take the sheep out to the downs without human help, and they could bring them back to shelter. They knew the sheep in their own flocks, and could distinguish them from the sheep in other flocks. As with the Iceland Dog, they could also herd the ponies. This

Lorna Irvine Burgess, shown in these studies with some of her Shetland Sheepdogs, is a granddaughter of Alexander Irvine, one of the founders of the breed. Mrs. Burgess's Hjatland Kennels, located in Robin's Brae, Dunrossness, in the Shetland Islands, is the oldest Sheltie kennel in existence. *H. Peace*

was necessary at times. Moreover, in times of food scarcity, the ponies would tend to come down to the gardens; the sheepdogs kept them out and sent them back to the grazing lands.

Life in the Shetland Islands has never been easy. Food has never been plentiful, and income has been low. The crofters had ponies instead of horses. And they had their small cattle (of which, today, not more than fifty exist). They could not afford large sheepdogs. And indeed, since the predators were gone, there was no need for a large dog. Enter, then, the ancestors of the Shetland Sheepdog.

(Left) James Thomason, far left, with unidentified companions, at a sheepdog trial in the Shetland Islands. (Right) This is a cross down from the "Yakki" dog, which would be crossed again with a smaller dog to further reduce size. James Thomason's daughter makes the friendly overtures.

3

Ancestors of the Shetland Sheepdog

T HE ERA of the purebred dog began about 1870. But most modern breeds can trace their exact ancestry no farther back than 1890 to 1910. In the years since 1870, enthusiastic breed specialists have been trying to trace their breeds back to the time of ancient Egypt. For the most part, they have simply stretched, bent and tortured facts and history in an effort to prove an ancient origin for their breeds. They have simply manufactured romantic lies about the origin of their dogs. It will not be the function of this book to concoct or perpetuate such lies.

We did make certain points in both Chapters 1 and 2. We pointed out that, so far as its mental capacity, its inherited instincts, aptitudes and its trainability go, the sheepdog is older than recorded history. Although many of the northern, or temperate zone, sheepdogs conform vaguely to type, type breeding did not develop until the recent past. And in Chapter 2 we showed that the difficult life in the Shetland Islands made a small working sheepdog a necessity.

That difficult life caused conformation breeding to arrive in the Shetland Islands very late. Still, since type or conformation breeding did begin, we need to ask ourselves what the Shetland Islanders had to work with. What was their basic stock?

More than two hundred years ago, naturalists such as the immortal Buffon considered that the shepherd's dog was the basic dog from which all others have sprung. The type of dog they had in mind, conformation-wise, was a medium-size dog belonging to the Spitz family of northern dogs.

The Picts, who lived in Shetland during the seventh and eighth centuries, brought with them sheep and sheepdogs. The dogs were undoubtedly of Spitz type. The Iceland Dog also is of Spitz type, and so was the dog of the Greenland whalers, a breed called "Yakkie." Both the Iceland fishing fleets and the Greenland whalers stopped at Shetland, going and coming. Their dogs accompanied them. It is worth noting that the Iceland Dogs, as the Shetland Dogs, herd ponies as well as sheep.

During the early part of the nineteenth century, the island dogs were called "Haad." They were much larger than the later dogs. And their purpose was to chase, throw and hold the wild sheep until the herdsman could secure it. But by 1850 Scottish shepherds had developed both Scotch Collies and Border Collies, together with the present methods of working sheep. The new methods made it possible for the Shetlanders to develop a smaller herding dog.

Still, the type of the Scotch Collie was much admired, and Shetland and Collie crosses were certainly made. But the Collie of 1850, or even of 1900, was not the Collie of today. It was close to modern type, but it was smaller. The standard in 1900 called for males to be twenty-one to twenty-four inches at the shoulder. These dogs were slightly larger than those of 1850, just as the modern Collie is two to four inches taller than its ancestors of 1900.

There is no doubt that great herding dogs from Scotland were taken to the Shetland Islands. Because of the islanders' demand for a small herding dog, it is likely that dogs of twenty-one inches or less at the shoulder were used. Border Collies had a maximum shoulder height of twenty-one inches. These great little performers were competing in sheepdog trials a scant half-dozen years after dog shows were established. By 1873 they had achieved national importance in Wales. The smallest of these may also have been taken to the Shetlands.

At any rate, by 1910 very small, Collie-type dogs abounded in the Shetland Islands. They have been described as mongrels. They were not, as far as their abilities were concerned. All that was required was to improve their type.

All over the world, the need for the shepherd's dog was declining. People everywhere were attempting to save the great herding dogs that they had developed. Population was declining in the Shetland Islands. Fewer of the crofters' wives and daughters were making yarn and weaving "Shetland" products. Breeders in Scotland and in England were developing very beautiful Collies. The Shetland Islanders could not do otherwise.

Enter, then, the Shetland Sheepdog.

4

Establishment
of the Breed

T HE SHETLANDERS could not escape the worldwide ferment
to save native breeds from extinction. Their little sheepdogs performed so mar-
velously well that they had also become very popular among herdsmen in the
northern sections of the Scottish mainland, around Dundee, Inverness and Wick.
As early as 1900, efforts to save and purify the breed had begun.

One of the earliest breeders was Alexander Irvine of Vatchley, Shetland.
By 1902 he had firmly established a kennel. He called it Hjatland, after one of
the Norse spellings of Shetland. It was history's first Shetland Sheepdog kennel,
and it has remained continuously in operation ever since. Today it is operated by
Mrs. Lorna Irvine Burgess, Alexander's granddaughter, at Robin's Brae,
Dunrossness, Shetland.

In 1905 the Rev. H. B. Oddy arrived in Shetland to take over a parish
near Lerwick. He traveled widely on Mainland and the other islands. English
parsons had long played an important role in the preservation of hunting
sports, and in writing upon dog subjects of all kinds. Rev. Oddy was one of
them. He became acquainted with Alexander Irvine. And he watched the island dogs—called variously Toonie Dogs, Peerie Dogs and sometimes Shetland Collies—herd sheep and ponies. He also watched the dogs work on the
Scottish mainland.

In 1907 an effort was made to bring ''Shetland Collies'' to public notice by
providing classes for them at agricultural shows. In August of that year, an
advertisement appeared in the *Shetland Times*. It announced that classes would

be held for Shetland Collies at the coming Lerwick Fair. C. Lennie, Esq., of Scalloway, offered a prize of ten shillings for the "best Shetland Collie dog or bitch."

The *Shetland Times* for Saturday, October 31, reports the judging of the Shetland Collies. There were sixteen entered. The winner was a black and tan male named Sailor Bob. He was owned by A. Conley of Hill House. The name, Sailor Bob, may be significant. Many of the Shetland Collies went to sea on the fishing ships. And as we shall see later, a seagoing Collie played an important part in the breed's conformation.

Let us return to the Rev. Oddy. He was so impressed by the work of the Shetland Collies that he wrote an article about them. This appeared in the English magazine *Country Life*. The *Shetland Times* saw the article and reprinted it in full on April 25, 1908. We reprint it here.

> Novelties of the canine world are continually appearing, and the latest is the arrival of the Shetland Collie. The breed is very little known outside Shetland, though during the last few years a number of small kennels have been formed in Scotland. Classes have been allotted to them at several Scottish shows. And at the Dundee show in March last, an effort was made to form a club, and if possible to obtain recognition from the Kennel Club.
>
> Whether the breed has any real claim to be called the Shetland Collie is open to question, to my mind. I lived for nearly three years near Lerwick, and during that time went about a great deal, but never heard them spoken of as Collies. They were simply "peerie dogs." That they will do the work of the ordinary sheepdog is certain, and that they resemble the Collie in miniature cannot be denied. In coat, body, legs, feet, tail, and in fact in everything but the head and ears, they are a replica of the modern Collie.
>
> The eye is larger, and the head shorter and thicker than that of the Collie today, but very much like the head of the Collie of thirty years ago. The ears are erect but this may be easily altered if those who are interesting themselves in the breed think it advisable. The colours are white and sable markings, sable, sable and white, tricolor, black and tan, and the blue marl. In weight they vary from six pounds to ten pounds.
>
> Where the breed is known, it is very popular and there is a brisk demand for good specimens. They are pretty, intelligent, and very hardy. I believe that, hitherto, they have been bred rather by accident than by design. When the proposed club is formed, and fanciers take up the breed in earnest, any objectionable points will doubtless be bred out.

The Rev. Oddy's article had an almost immediate effect. The *Shetland Times* for November 21, 1908, carried this announcement:

> For some considerable time now, the small class of dogs described as "Shetland Collies" has been attracting attention, the dog being a general favourite. With a view toward preserving the purity of the breed, and improving it, a meeting of those interested will be held in the County Hall on Monday evening for the purpose of forming a "Shetland Collie Club."

The historic meeting was held on Monday, November 23, 1908. Provost Porteus, chief magistrate of the county, acted as chairman. J. A. Loggie, who kept a public house or pub, announced that he was the person who had called the meeting. Here is the report, as it appeared in the *Shetland Times*.

Mr. J. A. Loggie, Royal Bldg., said he was responsible for calling the meeting together. . . . He stated he had been in communication with the secretaries of the Aberdeen Kennel Club, The Toy Dog Society, and the Scotland Canine Society, from whom he had gotten copies of rules and other information that would be useful to their club.

It was moved by Loggie that a club be formed, and seconded by A. J. Jamieson of Scalloway. It was passed unanimously. The patronesses of the new club are Lady Marjory Sinclair, wife of the secretary for Scotland; Mrs. Alex Moffatt, Falkirk, wife of Sheriff Moffat, and formerly of Lerwick. The patrons are the Hon. J. Cathcart Watson, member of parliament for Zetland County; R. H. Bruce of Sumburgh; and Sir Arthur Nicholson, Bart. [Bart. is the abbreviation for baronet, the lowest hereditary title.]

The Honorable Presidents are Provost Porteus, Baillie Laing, and the Rev. A. J. Campbell. The committee is made up of A. J. Jamieson, Laurence Laurenson, Thomas Henderson Jr. of Spiggie, John Smith, Alexander Irvine of Vatchley, P. MacDougall, A. Nelson of Gott, J. W. Laurenson, Arthur Conley, William Manson, W. P. Harrison, and William Sinclair.

It was announced that the demand for the dogs is greater than the supply. It is necessary to form a stud book. A membership fee of two shillings, six pence per annum will be charged.

On December 12, 1908, the *Shetland Times* reported on the next meeting, at which the stud book had been officially set up. Here is the report of that meeting.

No dog shall be eligible for admission unless it complies with the standard laid down, and the owner's name, and the names of the sire and dam, date of birth, etc., be furnished. A charge of six pence shall be made for such registration.

The next business was consideration of the standard, when it was agreed that the type and points of the Shetland Collie shall be similar to those of the rough Collie in miniature. That the height of the Shetland Collie shall not exceed 12 inches, nor the weight, 14 pounds.

The following sub-committee was appointed to examine, measure, and weigh all dogs put forward for entry into the stud book. Thomas Henderson and Alexander Irvine for the south part of the islands; and John Smith, J. W. Laurenson, W. J. Greig, F. Hunter, and J. A. Loggie for the rest of the islands. There were 30 members enrolled.

Provost Porteus served as the first president and J. A. Loggie as the "Honourable Secretary." However, Collie breeders everywhere fought the new group and breed. They objected to the name Shetland Collie, and to the Shetland Collie Club. Finally, the name was changed to Shetland Sheepdog. It has kept this name ever since.

There now came agitation for recognition of a taller dog. First, Shelties were being bred and raised on the Scottish mainland, and even in England. And as a Shetland Islands authority recently told the author: "Our cattle, dogs and

Three generations of English champion bitches: (from left) Chs. Riverhill Rare Gold, Riverhill Rarity of Glenmist and Sypay Star of Glenmist. *Thompson*

Ch. Dilhorne Blue Ninth, a memorable winner in England. *C. M. Cooke & Son*

ponies seem to lose many of their native characteristics when bred away from Shetland. Perhaps removal to an easier climate is a factor. We only know that it happens.''

Another factor was the undoubted crossing with small rough-coated Collies. James Thomason, who joined the Shetland Sheepdog Trials Association upon its formation in 1923, and who served as its president for twenty years, tells the story of a small, good-looking Collie that lived for some years on a fishing ship that traveled between Iceland and Shetland. The dog was named ''Scott'' after the master of the ship.

Scott was finally put ashore at Lerwick. But he always seemed to know when ''his ship'' was in. He would greet it joyously, and would stay on deck so long as it stayed in harbor. Since Scott had the freedom of Lerwick, he mated with many of the island bitches. Thomason, who remembers J. A. Loggie quite well, believes that this Collie is in the background of Loggie's famous early winner, Lerwick Jarl.

After the name of the club was changed to Shetland Sheepdog Club, T. & J. Manson of the *Shetland News* office published the constitution and ''bye-laws'' of the organization. To illustrate the seriousness of the members, we quote here several paragraphs from it.

> That the Hon. Secretary shall keep a Register known as the Shetland Sheepdog Stud Book, wherein all dogs belonging to members of the Club shall be registered. In such Register must be inserted, if known, the name of the dog, the breeder's name, date of birth, names of sire and dam, and of grand-sire and grand-dam. A charge of 1/- shall be made for such registration. No dog shall be eligible for registration unless it is certified to be roughcoated, and at least 10 months old, and not exceeding 15 inches in height, measured from the ground to top of shoulder at highest point.
>
> That all members of the Club entering dogs for prizes offered by the Club at any Show, must have their dogs registered in the Club Stud-book kept for registration. And for shows of Agricultural Societies in Shetland, the register certificate must be produced at the time of making entry, and that the registered number, along with the dog's name, shall be entered in the catalogue.
>
> If for any reason the Club ceases to exist, the Cups, Trophies, Assets and Records belonging to the Club shall be placed in the custody of the Kennel Club, London, with the least possible delay.
>
> The Kennel Club, London, is the final authority for interpreting the Rules and Regulations of the Club in all cases relative to Canine and Club matters.
>
> No alteration or addition may be made to the Rules, Constitution of the Club, or Standard of Points, unless by the sanction of a majority of members, present at a Special General Meeting; the intimation of such proposed alteration must be made in writing to the Secretary at least one month before the date of the meeting, due notice of which shall be announced in the circular calling the meeting. Alterations shall not be brought into force until approved by the Kennel Club.
>
> The Club shall not join any Federation of Societies or Clubs.

It will be seen from all this that the Shetland Sheepdog Club had prepared itself for admission of its breed to championship classes at shows governed by the Kennel Club (England). And it had laid the groundwork for the worldwide popularity that was to come to the breed.

As was noted in Rev. Oddy's article, an effort had been made to form a Shetland Collie Club at Dundee. Nothing came of this at the time, although the project may have spurred the Shetland Islanders into forming their own club. But in 1909 the Scottish Shetland Collie Club was formed, with C. F. Thompson of Inverness as secretary. Thompson had founded his Inverness Kennels. Graham Clark had set up Ashbank. And Keith and Ramsay had founded Downfield. The club founded its own stud book.

Both clubs ran into immediate opposition at the Kennel Club, and by Collie fanciers. Both decided to retreat to the name Shetland Sheepdog. Thus in 1910 the Kennel Club invited both clubs to send representatives to the Kennel Club council in London. They did so as the Shetland Sheepdog Club and the Scottish Shetland Sheepdog Club.

The breed was not at that time given official recognition. That came in 1914, the year in which the English Shetland Sheepdog Club was founded with A. C. Shove as secretary. In the meantime, the Kennel Club did accept registrations. There were forty-eight Shetland Sheepdogs registered in 1910. The breed was listed in the miscellaneous class with such others as Iceland Fox Dogs, Potsdam Greyhounds, Siberian Dogs, Roseneath Terriers and Welsh Cockers. Maltese Poodles and Cairn Terriers were also listed. The former survives as the Maltese. But of the others, only the Shetland Sheepdog and the Cairn survive.

One of the great encyclopedias of the early part of the century was Sydney Turner's *Kennel Encyclopedia*. It was published in 1910, when Turner was chairman of the Kennel Club (England). James A. Loggie wrote an article for that encyclopedia. Since he was the first fancier of the breed to write about it, we close this chapter by quoting his article in full.

> That the Shetland Sheepdog is a distinct breed no one can deny. It was originally known as the Shetland Collie or Toonie Dog. The dog took its title from the fact of its being used to drive the sheep off the township croft, or what is known in Shetland as the "Toon." Many years ago, when the large sheep farms were established in Shetland, shepherds from the mainland brought with them Scotch Collies, and gave the progeny to the crofters. But in-breeding and the want of keeping up fresh blood soon caused the breed to become diminutive. Few people (who have not visited Shetland) are aware of the conditions of these crofts; very few of them have fences or dykes to protect their crops, or to divide arable land from the hill pasture; and in seasons when the hills are scarce in pasturage, the sheep come down and feed off the stacks of hay and corn in the stockyard, and also eat the turnips and cabbage growing around the house. When this occurs, the dog has a duty to perform, and is used to drive the sheep back into the hills, and need not be accompanied by its master when once it gets the order to go.
>
> When the dipping season comes around the owners of sheep on hill scattold meet on a given date with their dogs and combine to drive the sheep to the dipping places appointed. This is known locally as "caaing" or "driving."

Ch. Westwin Sail on Sailor, owned by Gordon and Michelle Malsbury.

Ch. Lynnlea Parade Dress (center) with two of his daughters, Water's Edge Catalina Isle (left) and Towne's Parade of Elegance. *Meneley*

17

The Shetland sheep, although small, are very wild, and they require a good deal of handling to bring them together. They are very agile, and a five foot wall does not deter them from getting out, if they want to.

The Shetland Crofter grudges keeping a large dog, principally on account of the food it requires, while the smaller one suits his purpose.

Years ago when Greenland whalers called at Shetland, the men belonging to those islands, who formed a part of the crews, brought with them what was known as the ''Yakkie'' dog, called after the natives of Greenland, who are known among the whalers as ''Yaks.'' Distinct traces of this dog (which was found useful to the crofters) are still to be found among the Island dogs.

These Yakkie dogs were bred with the Shetland dogs, and some of the strongest characteristics of the breed are often seen in the present Shetland dog, namely the black muzzle, large prick ears, and heavy brush of a tail, combined with a some-what foxy appearance.

The height of these dogs is usually 14 to 17 inches; but fashion, as in several other breeds, nowadays demands that these dogs should be bred smaller. This undoubtedly can be done; but like the building of Rome, cannot be expected in a day. In consequence of this desire for smallness, alien blood has been introduced, and with very unsatisfactory results, which have brought discredit on the native dogs. Fortunately, by the formation of two specialist clubs, the interests of the breed are now being more carefully looked after.

In breeding, type is of the utmost importance, and Collie character must be kept carefully in view. Meantime, the best and most typical specimens exceed the standard of height which is being tried for; but once type is properly fixed, height and weight may be arrived at. The colours usually met with are black and white and tan; black, tan and white; black; sable; and sable and white.

They are very affectionate and faithful, and no kinder or more lovable dogs exist. They attach themselves readily to children and are never treacherous. They require little food and attention. They are hardy, and can live in outdoor kennels when required to. They are not prolific, having generally litters of about three or four; strange to say, females invariably predominate, being generally two to one. They are fleet and can stand a hard day's running well.

In 1908, the Shetland Sheepdog Club was formed, followed by the Scottish Shetland Sheepdog Club in 1909. The combined membership is about 150. In 1909, the Kennel Club agreed to recognize the breed and registered the titles of both clubs. The Shetland Sheepdog Club standard of height was 12 inches and weight, 14 pounds, while the Scottish Shetland Sheepdog Club's standard of height was the same, but that of weight was 12 pounds. The clubs have done a great deal to popularize the breed and to stamp out alien blood. Any dog showing signs of Spaniel blood should be carefully barred.

The Shetland sheep is a very small animal, only about half the size of the Scotch black-faced sheep. It is not, therefore, necessary to have so large a dog to herd and keep them in bounds as is required in the Highlands. The Shetland Sheepdog is purely a crofter's dog, and those who own 10 to 30 sheep will not have any other. Those shepherds, however, who have 30 to 700 black-faced ewes have larger dogs.

One will find much of a contradictory and confusing nature in this chapter. And one can smile a bit at Loggie's brave words at the beginning of

18

his article. Perhaps he was anticipating a bit when he wrote, ''That the Shetland Sheepdog is a distinct breed no one can deny.'' And particularly since he and other breeders were introducing Collie blood. But what is undeniable is that the breed was on its way. And Loggie and his 150 colleagues made it possible.

Ch. Lynnlea Forever Amber, CD, owned by Ray and Dorothy Christiansen, was Best of Breed at the American Shetland Sheepdog Association Specialty in 1983, scoring from the Veterans' class at eight years old. She is also the dam of the Best-in-Show-winning Ch. Lynnlea Parade Dress.

5

First Standards
of the Breed

J AMES THOMASON remembers James A. Loggie well. Loggie moved to Australia, but his influence on the Shetland Sheepdog was great. Thomason remembers that there was considerable opposition to some of the methods used by Loggie. Primarily, this involved his breeding methods. Loggie remembered the Rev. Oddy's criticism of the head. And he felt the head could be improved by crossing the Shetland dogs with small Collies.

This he did, and his dogs were improved in head. But they were also larger than the twelve inches at the shoulder mentioned by Rev. Oddy. Loggie's ideas prevailed. But here let us quote Thomason directly.

> Some of his dogs were the very foundation of the breed, such as Lerwick Hakon, Lerwick Jarl, Lerwick Olaf, and Zesta. The latter was a sable and white bitch which was a sensation at Cruft's Show in London in 1913. Had it not been for his efforts, backed by the Lerwick Club, I doubt that the breed as we know it today would have come into existence.

The Shetland Sheepdog Club at Lerwick set up the first full standard of the breed. It did this in 1910, at the time it had decided to yield and change the breed's name from Shetland Collie to Shetland Sheepdog. T. & J. Manson of the *Shetland News* office printed the standard in booklet form. Through the courtesy of Lorna Irvine Burgess, we are able to print it here.

STANDARD OF POINTS OF THE SHETLAND SHEEPDOG

1. The SKULL should be as nearly as possible flat, moderately wide between the ears, and gradually tapering towards the eyes. There should only be a slight depression at stop. The cheeks should not be full or prominent.
2. The MUZZLE should be of fair length, tapering to the nose, and should not show weakness, or be snippy or lippy. The nose must be black, whatever the colour of the dog may be.
3. The TEETH should be sound, and nearly as possible level. Very slight unevenness is permissible.
4. The JAWS clean cut and powerful.
5. The EYES should be of medium size, set somewhat obliquely and close together, of almond shape, and of brown colour—full of intelligence and expression.
6. The EARS should be small, and moderately wide at the base, and placed fairly close together on top of skull. When in repose they should be thrown back, but when on the alert brought forward and carried semi-erect, with the tips drooping forward.
7. The NECK should be of fair length, somewhat arched, and in proportion to the body.
8. The BODY should be moderately long and level with well-sprung ribs and strong loins; chest deep.
9. The FORELEGS should be straight and muscular, and with a fair amount of bone.
10. The HINDLEGS should be muscular at the thighs, with well-bent hocks.
11. The FEET should be oval in shape, soles well padded, and the toes arched and close together.
12. The TAIL should be moderately long, with abundant hair, carried low when the dog is quiet, with a slight upward swirl at the end, but gaily carried when the dog is excited, but not over the back.
13. The COAT must be double—the outer coat consists of hard hair; the under coat, which resembles fur, is short, soft, and close. The mane and frill should be abundant, the mask or face smooth, as also the tips of the ears. The forelegs well feathered, the hindlegs above the hocks profusely covered with hair, but below the hocks fairly smooth.
14. Any COLOUR except brindle is permissible.
15. The GENERAL APPEARANCE of the Shetland Sheep-Dog is that of the rough-coated Scotch Collie in miniature (Collie character and type must be adhered to). The height of the Shetland Sheep-Dog shall not exceed 15 inches at maturity, which is fixed at 10 months old.

Short nose; domed skull; large drooping ears; weak jaws, snippy muzzle; full or light eyes; crooked forelegs; cow hocks; tail carried over the back; under- or over-shot mouth.

Scale of Points

Head and Expression	15
Ears	15
Neck and Shoulders	5
Legs and Feet	10
Hind Quarters	10
Back and Loins	5
Tail	10
Coat and Frill	15
Size	15
TOTAL	100

Let us compare this with the Collie standard of 1907:

Height of dogs, 21 to 24 inches; bitches, 19 to 21 inches; measured at the shoulder. Colors: sable; black and tan; black, tan and white; blue or red merle; other colors permitted provided the dog has Collie characteristics. General appearance: A strongly made dog with a fair amount of bone, built on racing lines, lithe and active. The expression highly intelligent, the eyes small (slightly almond shaped) and dark in color.

The head rather long, without being exaggerated; flat on the skull; the muzzle fine, and tapering gradually to the nose, and well filled in—not falling away— under the eyes. The ears set on high, and should be very small. They should be carried semi-erect, with the tips inclining forward when the dog's attention is attracted and thrown back on the hair of the neck when running. The teeth should be sound and strong, and the mouth level. An over-shot or under-shot mouth is a bad fault.

Some Collies are "wall" or "China" eyed. This is more often found in the blue merle dog; it is quite correct and gives a particularly pleasing expression. [Such dogs are often preferred by some old shepherds who hold to the superstition that a wall-eyed dog never loses its sight when it gets old.] The body should be of moderate length, well ribbed up; back, strong; chest, deep; neck, long; and shoulders fine. The forelegs should be straight, with plenty of bone; the feet oval in shape with hard, strong pads; hind legs strong; the stifle joints should be well bent with the hocks let down.

The coat is of the utmost importance as the dog has to endure all kinds of weather—snow storms, rain and gales, and the Scotch mists so prevalent in the Highlands. The outer coat should be of coarse hair, very abundant, dense, and straight. The under coat should be short, soft, and lie close to the skin. The frill around the neck should be very full and profuse, and extend to behind the shoulders. The back of the forelegs should be well feathered, but the hind legs should be free from feather. The brush should be shaped like that of a fox; but it is more fully coated. It should be carried down, reaching to within a few inches of the ground, and never carried curled over the back. When the dog is excited, however, it may be carried slightly higher than usual.

The principal faults were listed as large ears, prick ears, ears set too low and carried down; thick, coarse head; large, full eyes; weakness in body properties generally; forelegs out at elbow; curly or soft coat, or a thin, open coat, lack of undercoat; over-shot mouth or under-shot; brush carried over the back, or possessing a kink; and cow hocks.

This, then, is a description of the dog that served as a model for the Shetland Sheepdog. It is noteworthy that, at least at that time, wall or blue eyes were permitted in all colors, and that some even preferred this color. The accent on coat was a major part of the Collie, which had to face the gales of the Scottish Highlands. And the little Shelties had to face even worse storms, and nearly constant gale winds. It is no wonder that the early standards thus specified a Collie coat.

Now let us return to the Scottish Shetland Sheepdog Club. Upon its organization in 1909, it had some forty members. And they had their own ideas as to what a Shetland Collie should be. Their club standard called for a dog that is, in appearance, an ordinary Collie in miniature; height about twelve inches; weight ten to fourteen pounds.

These were, of course, frustratingly vague requirements. They inevitably stimulated controversies. What is an ordinary Collie? Is it a run-of-the-mill farm dog, a moderately successful show winner or a champion? Does "about twelve inches" permit a dog to be only fractions of an inch away from twelve inches? Could one be only ten inches, or another fifteen? Moreover, the Scottish Club split the breed into rough-coated and smooth-coated varieties.

In 1913 the Scottish Club altered the standard to make "twelve inches ideal." But this only added to the problem. How tall or how small should a dog be before it is penalized for being too far from the ideal? These questions are not lightly asked here, nor were they in 1913. And they continue to frustrate breeders and judges alike in other breeds. For example, the present Pug standard says: "Weight from fourteen to eighteen pounds (dog or bitch) desirable." One Pug champion was officially measured at twenty-six pounds.

In 1914 the English Shetland Sheepdog Club was founded with A. C. Shove as secretary. The following year, Miss J. Wilkinson, a great breed pioneer, became secretary. The English club also had the concept of small Collie in mind. Its standard read:

"The general appearance of the Shetland Sheepdog is approximately that of the Show Collie in miniature." And again, twelve inches was given as the "ideal height."

That word "approximately" was to cause bitter argument for more than a decade. It was one reason for the formation of a second English club, the British Shetland Sheepdog Breeders' Association. This club, though active and successful for a time, did not survive. Most of the members finally returned to the original club.

Ch. Sheltieland Laird O'Page's Hill.   *Brown*

It was argued that ''approximately'' means only similar. But many breeders wanted an exact Collie in miniature. Others argued that an exact Collie in miniature was impossible. Still others argued against the fineness of the Collie head. Some wanted only a superior working dog that would resemble a Collie.

At the time the English Club was being formed, the Scottish Club altered its standard to make it more specific in some points. It now stated:

> Appearance: That of the modern Show Collie in miniature (Collie type and character MUST BE ADHERED TO). Ideal height, 12 inches at maturity, which is fixed at 10 months of age.

The attempt to produce a smooth-coated Shetland Sheepdog was also abandoned. Since 1914 there has been no such thing as a smooth-coated Shetland Sheepdog.

Even as late as 1914, attempts were made to call the breed the Shetland Collie. The insistence of breeders that the Sheltie be a Collie in miniature was perhaps an adequate reason. And the dog really did do the work of the Collie. But all attempts failed. The breed was, at times, classified as a toy dog. But later it was placed where it belonged, in the working group. Today, Shetland Sheepdog breeders object just as strenuously to the still-used ''Toy Collie'' as Collie breeders once did to ''Shetland Collie.''

6

Modern Breed Standards

IN THE PRECEDING CHAPTER, we discussed the problems faced by breeders, both in establishing a breed and in developing a workable standard for it. Now the Shetland Sheepdog is well established as one of the world's most popular breeds. Since it has spread around the world, breeders have developed in each country. Conditions vary from country to country, and so do the ideas of the breeders. But the standards that they adopt are quite similar.

We are chiefly interested in the Shetland Sheepdog in North America—in the United States and Canada. Since the standards are almost identical, we are printing in full the American standard. But we are adding some information on those of England and Australia. The present American standard was approved by the American Kennel Club May 12, 1959; the Canadian standard in 1962.

When the Canadian standard was approved, it called for the disqualification of any male over twelve months of age which had neither, or only one, testicle descended into the scrotum. Canada later passed a general rule to conform to the American rule which disqualifies a monorchid or cryptorchid at any age.

Perhaps we should be more specific in this. Correct medical terminology calls a dog with only one testicle descended into the scrotum a unilateral cryptorchid. If neither has descended, the condition is called bilateral cryptorchidism. But dog people usually speak of monorchid (one testicle descended) or cryptorchid (neither descended). The Australian standard does not mention the condition.

The English and Australian standards state that the ideal height for a male is fourteen and one half inches, and for a bitch, fourteen inches. The Australian standard adds that "anything more than one inch above these heights shall be considered a serious fault." The British standard also lists a weight of nine to sixteen pounds. It is noteworthy that the Australian standard ignores seriously undersize dogs. It is considered only a serious fault for dogs to be over fifteen and one half inches and bitches over fifteen.

In the United States and Canada, brindle color brings disqualification. It is permitted in England and Australia, even though serious breeders might frown upon it. The Americans and Canadians are also much opposed to the so-called degenerate colors, such as pale sable and faded blue, and self-color in blue merles. They also severely penalize dogs with more than 50 percent white body color. Other kennel clubs are less particular.

These points are worthy of note because Americans and Canadians import dogs from many parts of the world. They have always imported from the British Isles. But occasionally dogs are imported from Australia or New Zealand, or from continental Europe. It should also be remembered that Great Britain has now relaxed the rule that formerly disqualified monorchids. North Americans must, therefore, be very careful not to import such a dog. It might be a great winner in England, yet be disqualified and condemned for breeding in the United States and Canada.

Here is the American standard:

Preamble—The Shetland Sheepdog, like the Collie, traces to the Border Collie of Scotland, which, transported to the Shetland Islands and crossed with small, intelligent, longhaired breeds, was reduced to miniature proportions. Subsequently crosses were made from time to time with Collies. This breed now bears the same relationship in size and general appearance to the Rough Collie as the Shetland pony does to some of the larger breeds of horses. Although the resemblance between the Shetland Sheepdog and the Rough Collie is marked, there are differences which may be noted.

General Description—The Shetland Sheepdog is a small, alert, rough-coated, longhaired working dog. He must be sound, agile and sturdy. The outline should be so symmetrical that no part appears out of proportion to the whole. Dogs should appear masculine; bitches feminine.

Size—The Shetland Sheepdog should stand between 13 and 16 inches at the shoulder. NOTE: Height is determined by a line perpendicular to the ground from the top of the shoulder blades, the dog standing naturally with forelegs parallel to line of measurement. **Disqualification**—Heights below or above the desired size range are to be disqualified from the show ring.

Coat—The coat should be double, the outer coat consisting of long, straight, harsh hair; the undercoat short, furry, and so dense as to give the entire coat its "stand-off" quality. The hair on face, tips of ears and feet should be smooth. Mane and frill should be abundant, and particularly impressive in males. The forelegs well feathered, the hind legs heavily so, but smooth below the hock joint. Hair on tail profuse. NOTE: Excess hair on ears, feet, and on hocks may be

THE CORRECT HEAD

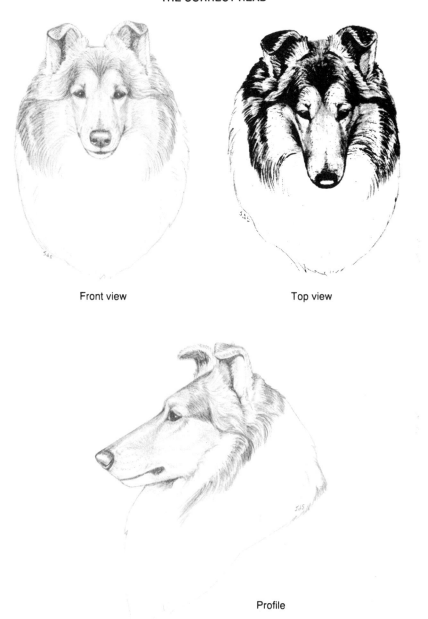

Front view   Top view

Profile

Drawings in this chapter—illustrating correct and poor heads, shoulder angulation, hindquarters, single tracking and trot—are by the noted artist Jean D. Simmonds.

trimmed for the show ring. **Faults**—Coat short or flat, in whole or in part; wavy, curly, soft or silky. Lack of undercoat. Smooth coated specimens.

Color—Black, blue merle, and sable (ranging from golden through mahogany); marked with varying amounts of white and/or tan. **Faults**—Rustiness in a black or a blue coat. Washed out or degenerate colors, such as pale sable and faded blue. Self-color in the case of blue merle, that is, without any merling or mottling and generally appearing as a faded or dilute tri-color. Conspicuous white body spots. Specimens with more than 50 percent white shall be severely penalized as to effectively eliminate them from competition. **Disqualification**—Brindle.

Temperament—The Shetland Sheepdog is intensely loyal, affectionate, and responsive to his owner. However, he may be reserved toward strangers but not to the point of showing fear or cringing in the ring. **Faults**—Shyness, timidity, or nervousness. Stubbornness, snappiness, or ill temper.

Head—The head should be refined and its shape, when viewed from top or side, be a long, blunt wedge tapering slightly from ears to nose, which must be black. **Skull and Muzzle**—Top of skull should be flat, showing no prominence at nuchal crest (the top of the occiput). Cheeks should be flat and should merge smoothly into a well-rounded muzzle. Skull and muzzle should be of equal length, balance point being inner corner of eye. In profile, the top line of skull should parallel the top line of muzzle, but on a higher plane due to the presence of a slight but definite stop. Jaws clean and powerful. The deep, well-developed under-jaw, rounded at chin, should extend to base of nostril. Lips, tight. Upper and lower lips must meet and fit smoothly together all the way around. Teeth level and evenly spaced. Scissors bite. **Faults**—Two angled head. Too prominent stop, or no stop. Overfill below, between, or above eyes. Prominent nuchal crest. Domed skull. Prominent cheekbones. Snippy muzzle. Short, receding, or shallow under-jaw, lacking breadth and depth. Overshot or undershot, missing or crooked teeth. Teeth visible when mouth is closed.

Eyes—Medium size with dark, almond-shaped rims, set somewhat obliquely in skull. Color must be dark, with blue or merle eyes permissible in blue merles only. **Faults**—Light, round, large or too small. Prominent haws.

Ears—Small and flexible, placed high, carried three-fourths erect, with tips breaking forward. When in repose the ears fold lengthwise and are thrown back into the frill. **Faults**—Set too low. Hound, prick, bat, twisted ears. Leather too thick or too thin.

Expression—Contours and chiseling of the head, the shape, set and use of ears, the placement, shape and color of the eyes, combine to produce expression. Normally the expression should be alert, gentle, intelligent and questioning. Toward strangers the eyes should show watchfulness and reserve, but no fear.

Neck—Neck should be muscular, arched, and of sufficient length to carry the head proudly. **Faults**—Too short and thick.

Body—In over-all appearance the body should appear moderately long as measured from shoulder joint to ischium (rearmost extremity of the pelvic bone), but much of this length is actually due to the proper angulation and breadth of the

POOR HEADS

Broad, round backskull combined with short muzzle giving "Pomeranian" appearance. Ears set too wide on skull. Eyes full. Lacking underjaw.

Snipey muzzle. Coarse, heavy cheekbones. Ears too large. Shallow underjaw.

High nuchal crest (occiput). Incorrectly breaking ears. Eye too small, beady expression.

shoulder and hindquarter, as the back itself should be comparatively short. Back should be level and strongly muscled. Chest should be deep, the brisket reaching to the point of elbow. The ribs should be well sprung, but flattened at their lower half to allow free play of the foreleg and shoulder. Abdomen moderately tucked up. **Faults**—Back too long, too short, swayed or roached. Barrel ribs. Slab side. Chest narrow and/or too shallow.

Forequarters—From the withers the shoulder blades should slope at a 45-degree angle forward and downward to the shoulder joints. At the withers they are separated only by the vertebra, but they must slope outward sufficiently to accommodate the desired spring of rib. The upper arm should join the shoulder blade at as nearly as possible a right angle. Elbow joint should be equidistant from the ground or from the withers. Forelegs straight, viewed from all angles, muscular and clean, and of strong bone. Pasterns very strong, sinewy and flexible. Dewclaws may be removed. **Faults**—Insufficient angulation between shoulder and upper arm. Upper arm too short. Lack of outward slope of shoulders. Loose shoulders. Turning in or out of elbows. Crooked legs. Light bone.

Feet (front and hind)—Feet should be oval and compact with toes well arched and fitting tightly together. Pads deep and tough, nails hard and strong. **Faults**—Feet turning in or out. Splay-feet. Hare-feet. Cat-feet.

Hindquarters—There should be a slight arch at the loins, and the croup should slope gradually to the rear. The hipbone (pelvis) should be set at a 30-degree angle to the spine. The thigh should be broad and muscular. The thighbone should be set into the pelvis at a right angle corresponding to the angle of the shoulder blade and upper arm. Stifle bones join the thighbone and should be distinctly angled at the stifle joint. The over-all length of the stifle should at least equal the length of the thighbone, and preferably should slightly exceed it. Hock joint should be clean-cut, angular, sinewy, with good bone and strong ligamentation. The hock (metatarsus) should be short and straight, viewed from all angles. Dewclaws should be removed. Feet (*see* forequarters). **Faults**—Croup higher than withers. Croup too straight or too steep. Narrow thighs. Cowhocks. Hocks turning out. Poorly defined hock joint. Feet (*see* Forequarters).

Tail—The tail should be sufficiently long so that when it is laid along the back edge of the hind legs, the last vertebra will reach the hock joint. Carriage of tail at rest is straight down or in a slight upward curve. When the dog is alert the tail is normally lifted, but it should not be curved forward over the back. **Faults**—Too short. Twisted at end.

Gait—The trotting gait of the Shetland Sheepdog should denote effortless speed and smoothness. There should be no jerkiness, nor stiff, up-and-down movement. The drive should be from the rear, true and straight, dependent upon correct angulation, musculation and ligamentation of the entire hindquarter, thus allowing the dog to reach well under his body with his hind foot and propel himself forward. Reach of stride of the foreleg is dependent upon correct angulation, musculation, and ligamentation of the forequarters, together with correct width of chest and construction of rib cage. The foot should be lifted only enough

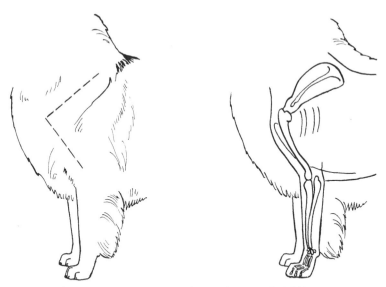

Correct: proper bone proportions and strong, straight legs.

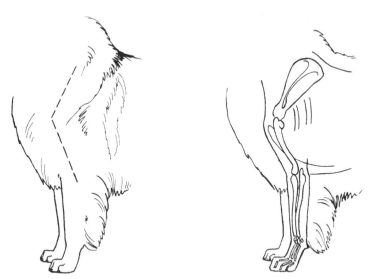

Poor: upper arm too short, shallow chest, weak pasterns.

 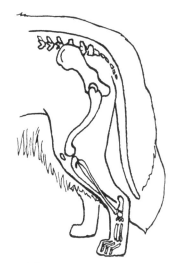

Correct hindquarters and tail. Proper leg angulation.

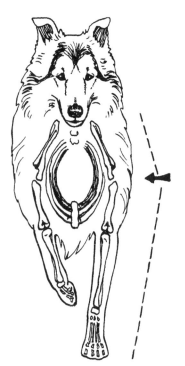 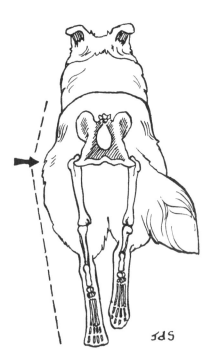

Correct position of single tracking, showing where proper break occurs. Legs are straight from breaking point to ground and are moving in direct line of travel.

to clear the ground as the leg swings forward. Viewed from the front, both forelegs and hind legs should move forward almost perpendicular to the ground at the walk, slanting a little inward at a slow trot, until at a swift trot the feet are brought so far inward toward center line of body that the tracks left show two parallel lines of footprints actually touching a center line at their inner edges. There should be no crossing of the feet nor throwing of the weight from side to side. **Faults**—Stiff, short steps, with a choppy, jerky movement. Mincing steps, with a hopping up and down, or a balancing of weight from side to side (often erroneously admired as a "dancing gait" but permissible in young puppies). Lifting of front feet in hackney-like action, resulting in loss of speed and energy. Pacing gait.

Scale of Points

General Appearance
Symmetry 10
Temperament 10
Coat 5 25

Head
Skull and stop 5
Muzzle 5
Eyes, ears, expression 10 20

Body
Neck and back 5
Chest, ribs, brisket 10
Loin, croup, tail 5 20

Forequarters
Shoulder 10
Forelegs and feet 5 15

Hindquarters
Hip, thigh, stifle 10
Hocks and feet 5 15

Gait
Gait—Smoothness and lack of
waste motion when trotting . 5 5

TOTAL 100

Disqualifications

Heights below or above the desired range, i.e., 13–16 inches. Brindle color.

APPROVED BY THE AMERICAN KENNEL CLUB MAY 12, 1959.

Those who check this standard against the Collie standard of 1908 will note many similarities. Apart from size, the modern Shetland Sheepdog standard is vastly more complicated. It also includes a "scale of points." Most breed clubs seem unable to eliminate such scales of points.

Yet dogs cannot be judged by mathematics. Those who have tried have usually made such a mess of it that exhibitors have been left screaming. Some standards have included a scale, but have warned that this is meant only to be a guide to the importance of the various parts of the dogs. In 1907 William Stephens, a Collie author and judge, remarked: "The judging or selection of Collies, or, for a matter of that, any other breed, by points, is not satisfactory."

Whether the Shetland Sheepdog scale of points has any value is open to question. A common complaint is that some judges concentrate upon finding good heads, and ignore rear ends and gait. Such judges are called "head hunters." It can be argued that the scale allows only twenty points for the entire head, and only ten for eyes, ears and expression. If one divides the ten into equal parts, then the ears would get three and a third points. Yet most judges would prefer to be shot rather than to give a winner's ribbon to a prick-eared dog.

On the other hand, the so-called head hunter might argue that only five points are allowed for hocks and hindfeet. A dog might have flat feet and cow hocks, and yet only five points could be taken off the score.

Temperament is a problem in Shetland Sheepdogs as it is in most breeds. The standard is reasonably clear on temperament, and states that the dog should not show fear or cringe in the ring. But the scale of points allows only ten points for this. One wonders if such dogs should be given ribbons.

In the previous chapter, we noted that controversy has always accompanied the formation of breed standards, as well as their later interpretation. In the case of the Shetland Sheepdog, there has been more controversy than with most breeds. A major modern point of argument has concerned size.

In the Shetland Islands, small size was important. The islands are poor, and have had increasingly difficult economic problems since about 1925. Sheep raising has diminished, and has tended to show fewer profits. So it was important to keep the dogs small. This was less true in other parts of Scotland and in England.

When brought to the United States and Canada, many dog breeds have tended to grow larger. Some have returned to parental size after a generation or two. Shetland Sheepdogs also tended to grow larger in North America. But because of the frequent early crosses with the larger Collies, they did not return to a smaller size.

The size controversy strongly erupted after World War II. The American Shetland Sheepdog Association wanted to alter the standard in many ways. It asked among other things for a height disqualification, both a minimum and a maximum. But at that time, the American Kennel Club opposed such disqualifications.

Moreover, Shetland Sheepdog breeders and owners were not unanimous on the issue. Naturally, breeders who had dogs that were over sixteen inches, or under thirteen inches, were opposed to any standard change that would disqualify their dogs. About 72 percent of the members of the American Shetland Sheepdog Association favored the disqualifying clause.

At that time, the secretary of the association was A. R. (Ray) Miller of Scarsdale, New York. Robert W. Orr was president, and Dorothy Allen Foster was vice-president. They led the battle for the disqualifying clause. So did Walter G. Miller of Bremerton, Washington.

Mr. A. Hamilton Rowan, secretary of the American Kennel Club, has supplied the writer with copies of the correspondence on the subject. The AKC had rejected the size disqualification in the proposed new standard. Walter Miller,

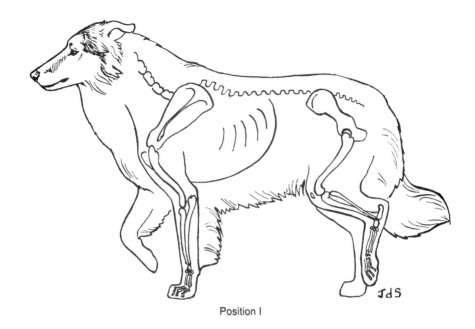

Position I

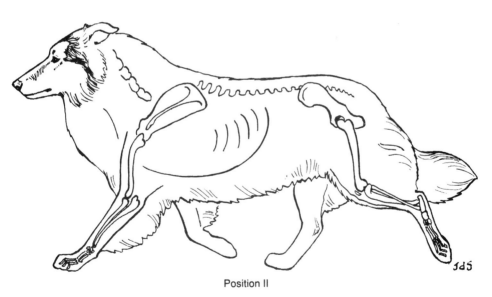

Position II

The correct trot: side view. Feet are lifted just enough to clear the ground. Free-flowing movement, with no apparent effort. Full reach in front with strong drive behind.

acting as a private breeder, strongly protested. His arguments were among those that eventually brought approval.

On June 12, 1951, Walter Miller wrote to John C. Neff, executive vice-president of the American Kennel Club, in response to an AKC decision disapproving the height disqualification clause in the proposed standard. Here are some pertinent quotes from Mr. Miller's letter:

> I will admit that it may be easier to get collie type in head and coat in the large Sheltie than in the small one. But who wants collie head type or runt collies? Or who wants all the collie weaknesses, including bad heads, weak jaws, cow hocks, and poor feet, that our breed has inherited from the collie crosses, both declared and otherwise? These things all throw back in the large dog, as well as a lack of brains and working ability.
>
> We wish to breed a small dog fifteen inches or under that can really work, and wish to have a standard of such a nature that we can breed this type for working and still enter the conformation shows with a chance of winning under judges who will consider soundness and type over lean skulls and draping coats of little practical value in bad weather.
>
> This is what we wish to get away from, the degeneration of our breed into a pretty toy that is useful only as a pet or bench show dog. If we don't keep the size down and breed for soundness, that is what we will get.
>
> There is a little Sheltie down in Colorado, under sixteen inches, who is the lifetime champion sheep dog of the state of Colorado. These are not AKC sponsored shows, but are contests promoted by sheep and livestock men who think their dogs are best and are willing to wager on them.

On June 28, 1951, Mr. Neff answered. We give excerpts from that letter.

> You present a very strong case for your contentions on size. This matter is never closed, Mr. Miller. If the American Shetland Sheepdog Association wishes to re-submit the Standard to us and support it with a presentation such as you make, I assure you that it would not be automatically disregarded on the theory that it was once examined. . . .
>
> Our board would not quarrel with extremely emphatic language as to height, just so long as it did not require actual disqualification of the dog. I think I may have made that clear in the letter which I wrote to the club. The administration of disqualifying faults is an extremely difficult one and it is the judgment of our Board that a Standard which calls for extremely severe penalties is ever so much more desirable than one which calls for outright disqualification.
>
> That does not apply in all cases. That is to say, our Board would never say that there should be no such thing as a disqualification in a Breed standard. It does look with real disfavor on a Standard which includes disqualification for more than a certain percentage of a certain color in coat, and it looks with considerable disfavor on a disqualification for height or weight alone. It is their view that severe penalties prescribed for variations from the ideal height should do more for the improvement of a breed than a mandatory disqualification which could be applied to an outstanding specimen which was measured out of the breed by so little as one-half inch.
>
> If the parent club can convince our Board that its general viewpoint on this matter is erroneous, I assure you that nobody would be disposed to be adamant.

Controversy? There you have it. Collie breeders were joining the ranks of Sheltie breeders. They had their own ideas. They certainly would not agree on the question of Collie brains. But, as Mr. Miller indicates, there were "head hunters" among both Collie breeders and judges.

The proposed standard had asked for a disqualification for dogs with 50 percent or more of white. This, along with the size disqualification, had been rejected by the American Kennel Club.

Following the Miller letter, the American Shetland Sheepdog Association conducted a winning battle for a size disqualification. In doing so, it paved the way for other breeds that have since placed height disqualifications in their standards.

But the battle against white color was at least partially lost. The AKC suggestion of a severe penalty was placed in the standard. This penalty has not only prevented predominantly white or heavily white spotted dogs from winning, it has also prevented the development of a white Shetland Sheepdog. The height and color provisions were included in the standard approved in March, 1952.

These four great Canadian champions are (from left): Ch. Simaril Vesta's Song, CDX, a BIS and HIT winner, Ch. Simaril The Wrapper and multiple BIS winner Ch. Simaril Tarna's Theme, all owned by Kathy Lovegrove; and Am., Can. Ch. Doreme's Branded Man, owned by Roselin Doss and Anne Power.

Hall

Ch. Beltane Notable, bred and owned by Paul and Barbara Curry.

7

Breed Recognition

AS EARLY AS 1910, the Kennel Club of England accepted registrations of Shetland Sheepdogs even though formal breed status had not been granted. There were forty-eight registrations, but the pedigrees were not published. We find no registrations for 1911 and 1912. In 1913, Miss Beryl Thynne registered a black, tan and white dog, Kilravock Laddie. He was whelped May 26, 1911, at C. F. Thompson's Inverness Kennel, a son of Inverness Yarrow and Inverness Topsy.

The English Shetland Sheepdog Club was founded in 1914, and in December of that year the Kennel Club granted full breed status for Shelties. There were sixty-four dogs registered, and five were exhibited, although before any challenge classes were available. All five were owned by Miss Thynne. The English Shetland Sheepdog Club standard differed from those of the earlier clubs and this is discussed in a separate chapter. What is important here is that the breed was now sufficiently advanced for recognition by the English Kennel Club.

While recognition had not previously been granted, still the Kennel Club had registered a number of kennels of breeders of Shetland Sheepdogs. These included Lerwick, owned by J. A. Loggie of Shetland; Ashbank, registered by Graham Clark; Downfield, owned by Mrs. J. C. Ramsay of Dundee, Scotland; and C. F. Thompson's Inverness Kennels. Also, during 1914, Miss Beryl Thynne registered Kilravock, and the Misses Grey and Hill were given the name of Greyhill. The following year, Miss E. P. Humphries registered Mountfort. And in 1917 Miss D. Macdougal Currie registered Bonheur.

Miss Currie's kennel was the last to be registered before shows were halted until the end of World War I. During the remainder of the war, breeding was by special license only. Three kennels which did keep going were Kilravock, Greyhill and Mountfort. That the breed survived is probably due to the dedication of these three kennels and their owners. When the war ended, the kennels had managed to save the foundation stock of the breed. They were able to augment their basic stock with dogs they discovered by scouring the Shetland Islands, Scotland and, to some extent, England.

If we could label a single dog as the foundation sire of the breed, it would have to be J. A. Loggie's Lerwick Jarl. He lived too early to have won a championship, but he was the grandsire of the breed's first two champions. Both won their titles just before shows were ended in 1917. Previous breed histories have credited Miss Beryl Thynne's Ch. Woodvold as being the first champion. Our own research indicates that the honor should belong to Ch. Clifford Pat.

During 1915 Clifford Pat, owned by the Misses E. Dawson and J. Wilkinson, won challenge certificates at Crufts, Richmond and Kensington. Woodvold won challenge certificates at Ladies Kennel Association and Westminster in England. He did not win a third until Southend-on-Sea in 1916 when he again won at Crufts.

Clifford Pat was born April 22, 1914. His breeder was W. Barnard. His sire was Clifford Sharper, a son of Lerwick Jarl. Woodvold's sire, Crichton Olaf, was also a son of Lerwick Jarl. Woodvold was bred by Keith and Ramsay, and he was whelped June 21, 1913. Frea, also a challenge certificate winner of 1915 owned by Mrs. B. Huband, was sired by Lerwick Jarl. Other challenge certificate winners of 1915 were Brittania of Kilravock, owned by Miss Thynne; Phoebe of Pix Hall, owned by the Misses Dawson and Wilkinson; Piggy, Misses Dawson and Wilkinson; and Shadforth Bretta, G. W. Hoggan.

Before shows ended in 1917, C. W. Higley's Taybank Uradale won a challenge certificate at Crufts, as did Nada, The Lily of Kilravock. The latter was sired by Ch. Woodvold, but the former by an unregistered dog. That year only seventeen Shetland Sheepdogs were registered, and only three were in 1918. The following year, there were twenty-two registrations.

By 1920 shows were once again well established, and the Shetland Sheepdog had managed to survive. Still, their numbers were few. During that year, Walesby Select won challenge certificates at Kensington and Crystal Palace. Four others won one each. They were Brenda, Starling, Foss and Hurly Burly, the latter owned by Miss Grey.

Then in 1921 Walesby Select became the first postwar Shetland Sheepdog champion. He won a third challenge certificate at Crufts, under judge H. Ainscough. His breeder was E. H. Phillips, and he was owned jointly by Phillips and Miss Beryl Thynne. He was by Kilravock Laddie, out of Shadforth Bretta, a 1915 challenge certificate winner that had once beaten Ch. Clifford Pat for best of breed. Ch. Walesby Select was sold to America. He has left little impression on the breed in either country.

Because their kennels made lasting contributions to the breed on both sides of the Atlantic, we are listing some of them.

Ch. Downfield Olaf of Walnut Hall.

Nutkin of Houghton Hill.

Ch. Eltham Park Ena.

Cameliard	Mrs. Allen and Miss P. M. Allen (later Mrs. Nicholson)	Helensdale	James G. Saunders
Clerwood	Dr. Margaret C. Tod	Houghton Hill	Mrs. Baker
Dryfesdale	E. Watt	Larkbeare	Clara Bowring
Eltham Park	E. C. Pierce	Netherkeir	A. Watt
Exford	Mrs. Sangster (daughter of Mrs. Baker)	Riverhill	The Misses Rogers
		"from Shiel"	Margaret Osborne

Mrs. Baker's Houghton Hill Kennels made major contributions to the breed for thirty years. Riverhill bred for nearly as long. The influence of Eltham Park on Shetland Sheepdogs in America is beyond computation. Mrs. Sangster, previously Mrs. Geddes, backed up her mother's kennels most successfully. Miss Osborne's "from Shiel" was registered in 1936. Her kennels are world-famous. Moreover, she is the author of the excellent English breed book, *The Popular Shetland Sheepdog*. Miss D. Macdougal Currie was for some years secretary of the English Shetland Sheepdog Club.

8

The Shetland Sheepdog Arrives in America

with Sue Ann Bowling

No ONE KNOWS when the first Shetland Sheepdogs reached America. Visitors to the Shetland Islands might have brought home "Shetland Collies" as pets long before the breed became fully established in either the Shetland Islands or in Northern Scotland. Such dogs would have left no impression in North America. Since so many Shetlanders immigrated to Canada rather than to the United States, it is likely that the first such dogs came to Canada.

John G. Sherman, Jr., of New Rochelle, New York, who also had an office on West Twenty-fourth Street in New York City, was the first to import registered dogs. His father had been the chief steward on a passenger ship sailing between Lerwick, Shetland, and Aberdeen, Scotland. Later, he managed the Queens Hotel in Lerwick.

Lerwick records show that the younger Sherman imported two dogs. One was Lord Scott, bred by A. Stephen of Aston Villa, Scalloway, Shetland. Lord Scott, erroneously listed as a bitch, was No. 61 in the stud book. He was whelped February 11, 1905, by Carlo, out of Daisy by Hero, and he was a pure golden sable.

The second was Lerwick Bess, bred by J. H. Hunter but owned by James A. Loggie. Bess was whelped September 8, 1908, a sable and white by Trim, out of Cary II by Winkie, No. 35 in the stud book. Lord Scott was sold to E. H. McChesney, who registered him in the AKC stud book.

Am., Can. Ch. Sandalwood's Midsummer Magic, owned by Yvonne Mariani.

Am., Can. Ch. Sherwyn Traces of Gold, bred by Fredna R. Pickerd and co-owned with her by Robert and Vicki Piccirillo. *Meneley*

Sherman bred Lerwick Bess to Lord Scott, and from this litter Mrs. K. D. McMurrich of Knaelcrest Kennels, Manotto, New York, registered Shetland Rose. The imports came over in 1910, and all three were registered in 1911. Sherman requested, and was given, permission to offer "The Shetland Sheepdog Club's American Challenge Cup" to be won three times by a dog or bitch for permanent possession. Lerwick Rex apparently won this trophy.

In 1912 eight dogs were registered, and four of these were direct imports. Since the breed was still young, the record of these is remarkable.

Alderbourne Kennels in England have been world-famous for nearly three quarters of a century. The author's father imported "two Pekingese Spaniels" from Alderbourne in 1906. And while Alderbourne is still noted primarily as a Pekingese kennel, it has had other breeds. Thus, Mrs. Ashton Cross of this kennel sent two Shetland Sheepdogs to the United States in 1911 or 1912. They were registered in 1912.

They were Jack McEwen, a black and tan, whelped April 9, 1910, and Sandy McPherson, a fawn and white, born February 28, 1910. Both dogs were pure Alderbourne breeding, which indicates that this kennel had been interested in Shelties for several canine generations at least.

By far the most famous of the dogs of 1912 was Lerwick Rex. J. G. Sherman imported him. He was by Berry out of Bee, and was bred by a Mr. Henderson of Lerwick, Shetland. He was whelped March 26, 1910, and was black and white. Sherman also imported Scalloway Belle. Belle was whelped May 22, 1910. She was bred by William A. Low of Shetland, and was by Trim out of Asta Flo.

These dogs were used extensively for breeding. Kenneth McMurrich had bought Shetland Rose for his wife. Rose was bred to Lerwick Rex, and she produced Lerwick Spot, Chucky and Sheltie. Mrs. T. D. McChesney bred Scalloway Belle to Lerwick Rex and got Lerwick Belle. Meanwhile, Mrs. W. F. Parker of Meriden, Connecticut, had brought over Sable. She was bred by W. H. Wilkinson of Shetland, and was a sable and white whelped October 23, 1909.

That year, 1912, Shetland Sheepdogs were shown at the Westminster Kennel Club show. Sexes were combined. Lerwick Bess was first, Shetland Rose second and Lord Scott third. Sexes were split at Nassau. Lerwick Rex was winners dog and Jack McEwen reserve. Lerwick Bess was winners bitch and Shetland Rose reserve. At Long Island, Jack McEwen was winners and Lerwick Rex reserve. Sable was winners bitch and Scalloway Belle reserve.

With the sexes combined at Ladies Kennel Association, Lerwick Rex took the points with Jack McEwen reserve. The results were the same at the Toy Spaniel Club, but Lerwick Bess took the bitch points, as she did at Plainfield, where Lord Scott was winners dog.

In 1913 twelve dogs were exhibited, but only three were registered. All three were of American breeding. In 1914 only three were registered. Mrs. Wilbur F. Parker of Meriden, Connecticut, registered Highland Laddie and Highland Lassie. And Mrs. Lillian Rague registered Lerwick Laddie. He was bred by Mrs. T. D. McChesney.

Ch. Lynnlea's Fortune Hunter, owned by Raymond and Dorothy Christiansen and bred by Nancy A. Wagner, was a Group winner from the classes. *Carter*

Ch. Shadow Hill's Jazz On Prin Hill, owned by Larry and Patricia Brunner. *Jan*

Lerwick Rex became the first champion of the breed in the United States, winning his title in 1915. It is odd that he should have won his championship in the same year that Clifford Pat became the first champion of record for the breed in England.

Mrs. McChesney had sold Lerwick Belle to Miss J. Fritz. The dog was shown in 1917, as was Lerwick Rex. But World War I was now in its third year. Breeding in the British Isles had been cut to a minimum, and dog shows were cancelled. The effect upon the Shetland Sheepdog was disastrous in the United States.

Only a dog called Daisy was shown in the United States in 1916. And Ch. Lerwick Rex and Lerwick Belle were the top winners among those shown in 1917. But breeding and importing had ceased. And it would be six years before interest in the breed revived in the United States.

The following numbers are the annual Sheltie registrations, starting in March 1909, from actual counts of Shelties registered in the *Kennel Gazette.*

Year	Number Registered	Number Traceable to Modern Shelties
1909	28	4
1910	62	9
1911	68	7
1912	70	6
1913	59	12
1914, through August	55	9
Total Before Separate Breed Status	342	47
1914, September on	17	1
1915	54	4
1916	44	8
1917	29	5
1918	4	0*
1919	23	6
1920	32	7
1921	82	23

* Decline due to World War I disruption and breeding restrictions

Offspring of unregistered parents, I believe, mostly from the Shetland Islands, continued to be accepted by the Kennel Club for registration well into the 1960s, and some of these are behind modern champions here and in the U.K. Therefore, the dogs traceable to modern American champions (right column) are by no means the complete foundation stock of the breed.

Many contemporary fanciers do not remember brace and team competition at the Westminster show, but in their heydey these contests were popular with spectator and participant alike. The happy winner of Best Team in Show at the 1940 Westminster was none other than Elizabeth D. Whelen with (from left) Ch. Bil-Bo-Dot Blue Flag of Pocono, Timberidge Truth of Pocono, Ch. Pentstemon of Beach Tree and Ch. Sea Isle Merle Legacy. Dr. Samuel Milbank was the presenter for the first of the five such awards Miss Whelen's dogs would receive over the next thirteen years.

9

Renewal of American Interest in Shetland Sheepdogs

IN JULY 1923 Mrs. Byron Rogers of Manhasset, Long Island, New York, registered two English imports. They were Kilravock Shrew of Misty Isles, a bitch bred by Miss Beryl Thynne, and Lady Park of Misty Isles, a bitch bred in England by J. G. Saunders. The former was by English Champion Walesby Select, out of Kilravock Naomi, a sable and white whelped July 31, 1921. The latter was also a sable and white by Rip of Mountfort out of Farburn Bo Bo, whelped June 16, 1921.

These two bitches made a tremendous impression upon those who saw them. One who liked the dogs was Edward R. Stettinius, Jr. In September he registered two imports that had been sent to him in care of Mrs. Rogers. These were Kilravock Lassie and the sire of Kilravock Shrew of Misty Isles, Eng. Ch. Walesby Select. Lassie was bred in Scotland by a Mr. Cusin. She was a sable and white, whelped October 11, 1922, by Irvine Ronnie out of Chestnut Lassie. Thus, on her dam's side, she came from one of the most famous bloodlines in the British Isles.

Walesby Select was bred by E. H. Phillips of Scotland, and was whelped June 1, 1919. He was by Kilravock Laddie out of Shadforth Bretta. He was inbred both to his sire and to Ch. Woodvold, one of the first pre–World War I champions. He won challenge certificates at the Kensington and Crystal Palace shows in 1920 and at Crufts in 1921.

In 1924 five Shelties were registered. One of these was Eng. Ch. Nettle of Mountfort, imported by R. E. Gregg. The breeder was Miss E. P. Humphries. The dog was a sable and white, whelped April 10, 1921, by the famous War Baby of Mountfort out of Christmasbox of Mountfort.

By this time, Kilravock Lassie had come into the possession of Catherine E. Coleman of Williamsburg, Massachusetts. She was bred to Eng. Ch. Nettle of Mountfort. From the resulting litter, Gregg registered Saucy Boy, Wee Man and Dusk. And Miss Coleman registered Prince of Whales.

Kilravock Lassie should probably be given credit for establishing the breed in America. This would not be so much because of what she produced, but because she started Miss Coleman in the breed. Her Sheltieland Kennels became one of the most famous in America, and it has existed longer than any other kennel in either the United States or Canada. Miss Coleman was the author of *The Shetland Sheepdog* and later, as Catherine Coleman Moore, of the revised edition, *The Complete Shetland Sheepdog*.

In 1926 Miss Coleman was given an imported male, Misty of Greyhill, born July 7, 1924, by Tarn out of Siria. Miss Fry brought over Eng. Ch. Eltham Park Esme. The following year, Miss Coleman imported Farburn Captain. He became the breed's first champion since Ch. Lerwick Rex in 1915. He was bred by W. M. Saunders, and was a sable and white, born October 28, 1924, by Forward out of Farburn Bo Bo.

Miss Fredericka Fry had founded her Far Sea Kennels at Cos Cob, Connecticut. Her Eng. Ch. Eltham Park Esme became an American champion in August 1928. Miss Fry understood that a successful kennel builds a foundation upon high-quality brood matrons. Esme had become a champion and now Miss Fry brought over a succession of excellent bitches from Eltham Park, the kennels of E. C. Pierce. Among her imports, not all bitches, were Eng. Ch. Eltham Park Ellaline, Eltham Park Bluette and, in 1928, Eltham Park Ensor of Far Sea.

The same year, Mrs. William F. Dreer imported Eltham Park Anahassitt. Mrs. Dreer had founded the Anahassitt Kennels, and these became nationally famous. Her new bitch was bred by E. C. Pierce. In addition, she brought over Merlyn of Cameliard, a dog bred by Mrs. J. A. and Miss P. M. Allen. He was by Eng. Ch. Eltham Park Eureka out of Aberlady Dot. It is interesting to note that Eltham Park Ensor of Far Sea was sired by Eltham Park Eurekason.

Homebreds were now beginning to appear. So in 1928 Kilravock Lassie was represented in registrations by puppies from two different litters. Wiggles, a son of Farburn Captain, was registered by Ellen B. Slater. And Miss Coleman, now of South Ashfield, Massachusetts, registered Black Eyed Susan and Sheltieland Sue. These puppies were by Misty of Greyhill.

In 1929 Miss Coleman imported Farburn Ellaline and Helensdale Lassie. Miss Fry brought over Eltham Park Eros of Far Sea, and registered a puppy, Rosette of Far Sea, sired by Ensor out of Esme. The following year Miss Fry imported Eltham Park Emmie of Far Sea, and Mrs. G. H. Edgell brought over

Ch. Sea Isle Serenade. *Shafer*

Ch. Rorralore Robert the Bruce.

Am., Can., Bda. Ch. Astolat Enchantor.
Shafer

Bushwave Baby Bunting. She was by Eltham Park Eurekason out of Brendagard by Eng. Ch. Walesby Select.

The famed Walnut Hall Kennels of Mrs. Katherine H. Edwards now appears. She registered Jock of Walnut Hall, a dog bred by Mrs. Dreer, and imported Downfield Olaf of Walnut Hall. Bred by J. C. Ramsay, Olaf was by Eng. Ch. Blaeberry of Clerwood—a dog figuring prominently in American Shetland Sheepdog history—out of Downfield Ethne.

Mrs. Dreer imported Ashbank Fairy, a sable and white also sired by Eng. Ch. Blaeberry of Clerwood, out of Ashbank Sheila. Downfield Olaf of Walnut Hall and Ashbank Fairy became American champions. In the meantime, William W. Gallagher, who founded the O'Pages Hill Kennels, had imported Helensdale Laddie, a full brother to Miss Coleman's Helensdale Lassie. He was an English champion and became an American champion. He was sired by the famed Chestnut Bud out of Aberland Wendy.

Here are the early champions in the order they won their titles:

1915   Ch. Lerwick Rex

1927   Ch. Farburn Captain

1928   Ch. Eltham Park Esme

1929   Ch. Wee Laird O'Downfield
        Ch. Eltham Park Ena (not registered)

1930   Ch. Downfield Grethe

1931   Ch. Downfield Olaf of Walnut Hall
        Ch. Ashbank Fairy

1932   Ch. Miss Blackie
        Ch. Mowgli
        Ch. Adorable of Anahassitt
        Ch. Bodachan of Clerwood
        Eng. Ch. Helensdale Laddie
        Ch. Sprig of Houghton Hill

1933   Ch. Piccolo O'Page's Hill
        Ch. Helensdale Sapphire
        Ch. Ariadne of Anahassitt
        Ch. Downfield Jarl
        Ch. Golden Girl of Walnut Hall (unregistered)
        Ch. Tilford Tulla
        Ch. Pegasus O'Page's Hill
        Ch. Tiny Betty of Walnut Hall

1934   Ch. Gigolo of Anahassitt
        Ch. Lady Tamworth O'Pages Hill
        Ch. Eltham Park Elyned of Far Sea
        Ch. Kim O'Pages Hill
        Ch. Alice of Anahassitt

Elizabeth Whelen with Victory of Pocono, CDX, and Ch. Larkspur of Pocono, CDX, making new friends for the Shetland Sheepdog.

Shetland Sheepdog fans have always supported their Specialties. Here at the Interstate SSC in 1953 a historic group shares the awards presentation. They are (from left) Constance Hubbard with the BB winner Ch. Frigate's Emblem of Astolat, judge Alex Gibbs and Elizabeth Whelen with the BOS Golden Sequin of Lillegard, owned by Vernon and Kay Johnson.   *Shafer*

1935   Ch. Coltness Commander
        Ch. Neilsland Nuffsaid
        Ch. Dancing Master of Anahassitt
        Ch. Tiny Chloe of Walnut Hall
        Ch. Peter Pan O'Pages Hill
        Ch. Anahassitt Aphrodite
        Ch. Promise O'Pages Hill
        Ch. Wee Cubby of Far Sea
        Ch. Sheltieland Thistle

Dogs that came after Ch. Lerwick Rex can be considered to be the true foundation stock upon which the subsequent history of the Shetland Sheepdog in America rests. Some additional information should be given about them.

Miss Catherine Coleman claims the honor of breeding the first America-bred champion. She bred Ch. Miss Blackie. She sent Ch. Sheltieland Thistle, the first blue merle champion, to English and American Ch. Helensdale Laddie, owned by W. W. Gallagher. Miss Blackie, one of the puppies from this mating, went to the ownership of Mr. Gallagher. As her name suggests, she was black, white and tan, whelped May 30, 1931. In May 1932, the American Kennel Club recorded her championship at about ten months of age.

During that same May, the championship of Mowgli was recorded. So Miss Blackie beat him out by only a couple of dog shows. And in July of 1932, the American Kennel Club published the championship of Adorable of Anahassitt. She, too, was American-bred. Adorable was bred by Mrs. William F. Dreer of Rosemont, Pennsylvania, and she was a tri-color sired by Ch. Wee Laird O'Downfield out of Natalie of Clerwood.

Ch. Sheltieland Thistle was owned by Catherine Coleman. She was the first blue merle champion; her official AKC registration lists her breeder as Mrs. James G. Saunders of Scotland. Thistle was by Montlethen Blue Prince out of Helensdale Lassie, and the latter was imported by Miss Coleman. Thistle was imported "in utero" and was whelped at Sheltieland Kennels, hence her name, Sheltieland Thistle.

Ch. Wee Laird O'Downfield and Ch. Downfield Grethe were full brother and sister, though Grethe was some fifteen months older than her brother. Mrs. Dreer imported Grethe in 1929, and Wee Laird a year later. Mrs. J. C. Ramsay was their breeder. It would be impossible to overestimate the influence they made on the breed through Ch. Mowgli.

His pedigree tells a great deal about how a breed is made. In those days, the modern Shetland Sheepdog type had not been fixed. Inbreeding was used when dogs of the correct type, or dogs with especially desirable characteristics, appeared. The simplest way to express the meaning of inbreeding is to say that it is a contraction of the words *incestuous* and *breeding*. A brother and sister mating is the closest incestuous breeding that is possible.

Mowgli's dam was Jean of Anahassitt, and she was the result of a brother-sister mating of Ch. Wee Laird O'Downfield and Downfield Grethe. His sire was

Ch. Wee Laird O'Downfield. Mowgli was whelped July 2, 1931. He was owned by William W. Gallagher of O'Pages Hill. Mowgli appears to have had quality hitherto undreamed of. Most breeders know that the British Isles have a six-month quarantine period for dogs coming from North America. This effectively prevents the shipment of most dogs from the United States to England. Yet Mowgli's son, Ch. Sheltieland Laird O'Pages Hill, was sent to England just before World War II. There, despite the war, the dog became a well-known sire. In England, he represented three of America's greatest early kennels—Sheltieland, Anahassitt and O'Pages Hill.

Ch. Mowgli.

Ch. Peabody Pan.

Ch. Wee Laird of Downfield.

10

Lines, Families and Foundation Sires

by Sue Ann Bowling

$\mathbf{T}$WO LINES in a pedigree are often considered of particular importance: the all-male line, also referred to as the top line of the pedigree, the tail male or the sire line; and the all-female line, also referred to as the bottom line of the pedigree, the tail female or the family. Both of these lines have been traced to unregistered stock for all English CC winners, and almost all American champions can be placed into the lines and families thus defined in England.

There have been seven sire lines in all, only three of which produced more than a handful of CC winners. The earliest of these three was line LJA, which included Lerwick Jarl and his full brother, Am. Ch. Lerwick Rex. Both are behind modern dogs through females. Although LJA was the dominant line prior to World War I, it was almost completely replaced by the Collie-cross CHE and BB lines by the late 1920s. The first registered dogs of lines BB and CHE were registered in 1914, but only BB had any representatives in the Stud Book prior to World War I, and the line that survives today comes from a dog bred while breeding was restricted during the war.

The BB line starts with the unregistered Butcher Boy through his son Wallace, registered in 1914. Wallace was bred in 1918 to the Collie Teena, to produce War Baby of Mountfort. War Baby sired Rufus of Mountfort, who was bred to the Teena daughter KoKo (by another Wallace son, Rip of Mountfort). This mating produced Eng. Ch. Specks of Mountfort. Specks, bred to the War

Baby daughter Princess of Mountford, sired Eng. Ch. Eltham Park Eureka. Eureka is behind all modern BB dogs through two sons: Eng. Ch. Max of Clerwood (who eventually went to the United States after siring Mordred of Cameliard) and Eltham Park Evolution. Mordred is behind Eng. Ch. Helensdale Ace, while Evolution sired Blinx of Clerwood, head of that part of the line behind the majority of modern English CC winners. Because the Teena cross was declared as a cross, the AKC refused registration to a number of excellent BB dogs, including Eureka himself. This together with the very limited use of the Eltham Park dogs imported by Far Seas Kennel helps account for the virtual absence of BB lines in the United States. (Note that the Eltham Parks did *not* have anything but a very minor influence on modern pedigrees.)

Line CHE takes its name from Chestnut Rainbow, who was bred to the Collie Chestnut Sweet Lady. The mating produced four dogs (Chestnut Bud, Redbraes Rollo, Nut of Houghton Hill and Chestnut Lucky Boy) and three bitches. All four dogs founded sublines, though only two or three are active today.

Chestnut Bud sired Eng. and Am. Ch. Helensdale Laddie, but this line was short-lived as a sire line, carrying on mostly through females.

Redbraes Rollo sired Eng. Ch. Gawaine of Cameliard, tail male to Am. Ch. Peabody Pan, a 1930s import to the United States that founded one of the two important CHE branches in this country. The first published genealogy charts in this country, covering the American champions from 1968 through 1970, showed this line as accounting for about a third of U.S. champions, including such outstanding dogs as Ch. Merrymaker of Pocono, CD/ROM; Ch. Merry Meddler of Pocono, CDX/ROM; Ch. Bil-Bo-Dot Blue Flag of Pocono, ROM; Ch. Pixie Dell Bright Vision, ROM; and Ch. Sheltieland Kiltie O'Sea Isle. Over the last twenty years the line has almost disappeared as a sire line, apparently because its most recent outstanding dogs have produced bitches as their best offspring. (Ch. Halstor's Peter Pumpkin, ROM, and Ch. Romayne's Sportin' Life, ROM, are heavily linebred on Kiltie through daughters, even though their sire line goes back to Chestnut Lucky Boy.) Pan Champions were still being finished in 1984, so the bloodline undoubtedly still exists. Ch. Peabody Pan contributes about 11 percent of modern pedigrees.

Nut of Houghton Hill was behind the modern English CHE line through his inbred son, Eng. Ch. Uam Var of Houghton Hill. Although weak compared with the modern BB line in England, it is still producing a couple of CC winners a year. Several important early imports came from this branch, but all lines from these imports come through bitches.

Chestnut Lucky Boy was bred to his litter sister Chestnut Blossom to produce Eng. Ch. Blaeberry of Clerwood. This dog overwhelmingly dominates U.S. pedigrees. He sired Am. Ch. Wee Laird O'Downfield, who makes up about 30 percent of modern U.S. pedigrees. He also sired Am. Ch. Downfield Grethe (about 6.5 percent), Am. Ch. Ashbank Fairy (about 7.8 percent) and Natalie of Clerwood (about 6.4 percent), and is behind other imports farther back in the pedigrees. The Wee Laird heads the tail male line to all 1989 Champions so far,

Ch. Frigate's Emblem of
Astolat. *Shafer*

Ch. Pixie Dell Epicure. *Shafer*

Ch. Wynsome Donka Class
Act, owned by Kathie Peterson.

as can be seen in the chart summarizing the lines to the 155 1989 champions published through the October *Show Records.*

The families also differ in English and U.S. dogs. The most active English families are minor or nonexistent in the United States while the most active U.S. families have almost died out in England.

Family 2 is active through imports Ch. Downfield Grethe (one 1989 Ch.), Eng. and Am. Ch. Eltham Park Elyned of Far Sea (11), Ch. Helensdale Marigold of Walnut Hall (12) and Ch. Ashbank Fairy (46). In Family 12, Wizbang Joy traces to two 1989 champions, Foldgate Biddy to nine and Lynette to eight. Family 3 comes through Kilravock Lassie, 3B through Dinah of Sedgemoor, 4 through Tilford Tessa of Sheltieland, 5 through Helensdale Lassie and her daughter, Ch. Sheltieland Thistle, 6 through Natalie of Clerwood and 10 through Ch. Helensdale Sapphire.

Line Family	U.S. 1	U.K.		
		80–84	85–88	80–88
BB	0	136	98	244
CHE	155	8	9	17
F1	0	9	3	12
F2	70	0	0	0
F3 (Chestnut Lassie)	5	0	0	0
F3B (Iseburgh Pansy)	1	2	0–3*	2–5*
F3C (Chestnut Sweet Lady)	0	10	4–7*	14–17*
F3 Total	6	12	7	19
F4	9	1	0	1
F5	24	16	8	24
F6	24	9	13	22
F8	0	20	17	37
F9	0	55	39	94
F10	3	0	0	0
F12	19	0	0	0
F13	0	9	10	19
F16	0	3	1	4
F24	0	10	8	18

* 1985–1988 Eng. CC winners are from *The Nutshell* (English Shetland Sheepdog publication), which gives lines and families but does not break down Family 3. This family is actually made up of three probably quite separate families. The original Family 3 has not had a CC winner since before World War II, so I assume the recent English F3s are 3B or 3C, probably 3C which is the more active line. 3B produced Am. and Can. Ch. Nashcrest Golden Note in this country before it was even recognized in England, but has been a male-producing family here.

11

American Shetland Sheepdog Association

INTEREST in the Shetland Sheepdog grew so rapidly in the United States that, by 1928, fanciers began to talk about organizing a parent club. In those days, the first club to be organized to sponsor and promote a breed would be considered to be the parent club of the breed by the American Kennel Club. This was true whether the founding group had purely local ideas and local membership or was national in scope.

Many clubs then—and now—hold annual meetings at the time of the Westminster Kennel Club show at Madison Square Garden. Some of these clubs hold their meetings in club rooms at Madison Square Garden itself. Others meet at nearby hotels. At the "old Garden," which has been torn down, dressing rooms for the various athletic teams often served as meeting rooms. One room was used by the press corps; the other housed the meetings of various clubs during the two-day show.

Thus it was that the organization meeting of the American Shetland Sheepdog Association was held in a dressing room at Madison Square Garden. The date was February 12, 1929. Less than thirty people attended. Of these, twenty-three became founding members.

Miss Fredericka Fry of New York City and Cos Cob, Connecticut, was elected president, Mrs. W. F. Dreer of Rosemont, Pennsylvania, was made first vice-president and A. A. Parker of Worcester, Massachusetts, second vice-president. Miss Catherine Coleman of South Ashfield, Massachusetts, was elected secretary, and George C. Carr of Reading, Pennsylvania, treasurer.

Ch. Brandell's Break-A-Way, owned and shown by the renowned professional handler J. Nate Levine, was BB at the 1958 ASSA Specialty.

Ch. Valdawn's Talk of the Towne, owned by Kathleen A. and Herbert S. Searle, was BB at the 1973 Westminster show under judge A. Raymond Miller. The handler was Barbara Kenealy.

Gilbert

The executive committee was made up of Mrs. Gladys Funke of New York City (she had served as temporary chairman of the meeting), Miss Gertrude Sampson of New York City, C. J. Spill of Garden City, New York, Oscar Day of Fulton, New York, and J. Edward Shanaberger of Ravenna, Ohio.

It is worth nothing that J. Nate Levine became one of America's top professional handlers. J. Edward Shanaberger became an all-breed judge, then turned to professional handling and finally left the sport of dogs to train trotting horses. Benjamin Richardson, also a founding member, was a professional handler from Cos Cob, Connecticut. So far as the writer remembers, he handled the dogs for Miss Fry, and at least for a time managed her kennel. Such early importers as Mrs. Byron Rogers, Edward R. Stettinius and Robert E. Gregg seem never to have been members of the association.

Several months after the association was founded, and after a meeting at the Boston show in early March, the club applied for membership in the American Kennel Club. The association had studied the constitutions of other clubs, and had adopted its own at the New York meeting. At the Boston meeting, it had formalized procedures for elections and other matters. Miss Fredericka Fry then presented the association's application to the American Kennel Club. Membership in the American Kennel Club costs $250. Miss Fry personally paid the fee.

Miss Katherine H. Edwards became a member of the executive committee in 1930, and Miss Katherine Lindsay in 1933. Miss Elizabeth D. Whelen became an executive committee member in 1936, and A. Raymond Miller in 1941. Mr. Miller died just after completing his 1973 Westminister Kennel Club judging assignment. Mr. Miller represented the American Shetland Sheepdog Association to the American Kennel Club for many years until his death.

Of course, national officers change from time to time. But the national association remains. Readers wishing to reach the officers can always do so through the American Kennel Club, 51 Madison Avenue, New York, New York, 10010.

Ch. Nicholas of Exford, owned by Mrs. H. W. Nichols, Jr., was BB at the 1936 ASSA Specialty show.

Brown

12

The National Specialty Show

A SPECIALTY SHOW is one for a specific breed, given by a breed club. The breed club can be the national parent club of the breed, or it can be a regional club. The club can give its own show, separate from any other. Or it might join a group of other breed clubs and form a specialty club's association. The association would then give a show for its member clubs. Finally, either a national or a regional club can designate the classes at an all-breed show as its specialty show. A regional club must, however, obtain permission for any kind of show from its parent club.

After its formation, the American Shetland Sheepdog Association grew strong enough to hold a specialty show. It decided to designate the classes at the Morris & Essex Kennel Club show as its specialty. This was a natural choice. Morris & Essex was the greatest outdoor show of its day. It was held in May when Shelties are usually in good coat. Thus, the association's first specialty show was held in May 1933, in conjunction with Morris & Essex.

Edward D. McQuown, who for many years was one of America's finest all-breed judges, officiated. There were fifteen dogs and eighteen bitches that actually competed. Tilford Tulla, owned by Mrs. W. F. Dreer, was winners dog. Ariadne of Anahassitt, also owned by Mrs. Dreer, was winners bitch and best of winners. Ch. Piccolo O'Pages Hill, owned by W. W. Gallagher, was best of breed. It is noteworthy that the winner of both the puppy and novice dog classes was Gigolo of Anahassitt.

The next year, William H. Schwinger, an officer of the famed Collie Clan of the Midwest, was the judge. This show, as were those of 1935 and 1936, was also held in conjunction with Morris & Essex. That year, Morris & Essex had 2,431 competing dogs. Gigolo of Anahassitt, now a champion, was best of breed and went on to place second in a strong working group to the Great Dane, Nero Hexengold. The group judge was Dr. T. D. Buck.

Today it is not usual for a champion to enter the open class. But they are not barred from doing so. Gigolo was entered in the open class, and so he went on to a group second from it. The winners bitch was Eltham Park Elyned of Far Sea, owned by Mrs. Fredericka Fry del Guercio. She had won both the limit and the open classes. There were eighteen dogs and twenty-four bitches in competition.

The 1935 show had 2,784 competing dogs—an amazing entry for that time—and there were nineteen Sheltie dogs and nineteen bitches competing. Joseph Burrell was the judge. Ch. Piccolo O'Pages Hill was best of breed, as he had been in 1933. Winners dog was Peter Pan O'Pages Hill. The great producing bitch of a later time, M. J. Kennedy's Keep Goin', was winners bitch and best of winners from the novice class.

The famed Dancing Master of Anahassitt was reserve winners dog, and Captivator Jenny Wrench, owned by E. S. Huhn, was reserve winners bitch. Oddly, she, too, had come from the novice class.

Nicholas of Exford, who later became a champion, was best of breed at the 1936 show. The next year, the specialty was moved to Cleveland. Again the judge was William H. Schwinger. His best of breed was Lady Precious O'Pages Hill, and she came up from the puppy class. She was owned by W. W. Gallagher. Kalandar Prince O'Pages Hill, also owned by Gallagher, was winners dog.

The 1937 show was notable for the great producing dogs and bitches that were entered in the classes—twenty-six dogs, twenty-five bitches and three for specials only. These were Tiny Margaret of Walnut Hall, owned by Mr. and Mrs. H. W. Nichols, Jr. (whose daughter, Tiny Margurite of Walnut Hall, was best of breed in 1940); Ch. Lady Tamworth O'Page's Hill, owned by Gallagher; and Ch. Dancing Master of Anahassitt. Ch. Mowgli, and the previous year's winner, Ch. Nicholas of Exford, an imported dog, were entered for exhibition only.

In the classes at that great show of March 13–14, 1937, were such all-time great dogs as Merrymaker of Pocono, China Clipper O'Pages Hill, Melchior of Anahassitt, Black Sachem O'Pages Hill, Ch. Gigolo of Anahassitt, Kelpie, Beach Cliff's Lizette (first Sheltie ever to win a Utility Dog obedience degree), Ronalee Norseman, Gregor MacGregor of Bagaduce and Ch. Ariadne of Anahassitt.

Ch. Gigolo of Anahassitt had won the second specialty show. He and Ch. Ariadne of Anahassitt were entered in the open classes at this show. It is hindsight, perhaps, but few shows in the history of the breed, or of any breed, could boast so great a group.

Ch. Pixie Dell Little Gamin, owned by Mr. and Mrs. A. Raymond Miller, was BB at the 1945 ASSA Specialty.

Brown

The year 1961 was yet another that was memorable for the Millers' Pixie Dell establishment; they took BB at the ASSA Specialty for their blue merle dog, Ch. Pixie Dell Royal Blue. *Norton of Kent*

1933	Ch. Piccolo O'Pages Hill
1934	Ch. Gigolo of Anahassitt
1935	Ch. Piccolo O'Pages Hill
1936	Ch. Nicholas of Exford
1937	Ch. Lady Precious O'Pages Hill
1938	Ch. Sheltieland Laird
1939	Ch. Kalandar Prince O'Pages Hill
1940	Ch. Tiny Margurite of Walnut Hall
1941	Ch. Will O'The Mill O'Pages Hill
1942	Ch. Victory of Pocono
1943	Ch. Windrush O'Pages Hill
1944	Ch. Timberidge Temptation
1945	Ch. Pixie Dell Little Gamin
1946	Ch. Timberidge Temptation
1947	Ch. Confection O'The Picts
1948	Ch. Creole Babe O'Pages Hill
1949	Ch. Noralee Autumn Gold
1950	Ch. Sea Isle Peter Pan
1951	Ch. Ald-A-Beth Flintlock
1952	Ch. Pixie Dell Theme Song
1953	Ch. Golden Sequin of Lillegard
1954	Ch. Nashcrest Golden Note
1955	Ch. Va-Gore's Bright Promise
1956	Ch. Va-Gore's Bright Promise
1957	Ch. Brandell's Break-A-Way II
1958	Ch. Dark Stream O'Pages Hill
1959	Ch. Mori-Brook's Country Squire
1960	Ch. Tiny Toby of Walnut Hall
1961	Ch. Pixie Dell Royal Blue
1962	Ch. Pixie Dell Bright Vision
1963	Ch. Tess's Trump Card of Wadmalaw
1964	Ch. Laurolyn Patti O'M. B.
1965	Ch. Elf Dale Viking
1966	Ch. Malpsh Great Scott

Ch. Mori-Brook's Country Squire, owned by Mori-Brook Kennels, winner of the 1959 ASSA Specialty.   *Brown*

Am., Can. Ch. Banchory High Born, owned by Kismet Kennels, took breed honors at the 1970 ASSA Specialty.   *Twomey*

Ch. Flair Peg O' My Heart, owned by Shirley Valo, made 1972 her year when she was BB at the ASSA Specialty.

Am., Can. Ch. Tiree Hall Jedelan Scot, owned by Mrs. Helen Hendrickson, added BB at the 1971 ASSA Specialty to his long list of good wins. *Olson*

Shown scoring at Interstate in 1954, both these Shelties were BB at the ASSA. Ch. Nashcrest Golden Note (left) was BB in 1954 and Ch. Va-Gore's Bright Promise did the same in 1955 and 1956. These dogs are shown with Elizabeth Whelen, Robert Wills and J. Nate Levine.

Shafer

Ch. Elf Dale Viking was one of the breed's most memorable winners. He was owned by Mr. and Mrs. Frank Sanders and handled by Wayne Baxter to a host of top awards. His wins include BB at the ASSA and the Northern California Specialties in 1965 and he is shown here in the latter presentation under Judge Elizabeth Whelen. *Bennett Associates*

Am., Can. Ch. Rorralore Sportin' Chance, CD, ROM, owned and handled by Charlotte Clem McGowan, was the top winner at the 1984 ASSA Specialty. He is shown here in a BB presentation at the Cleveland Specialty under the author. *Kotar*

73

1967   Ch. Malpsh Great Scott

1968   Ch. Halstor's Peter Pumpkin

1969   Ch. Lencrest Rebel Rouser

1970   Ch. Banchory High Born

1971   Ch. Tiree Hall Jedelan Scot

1972   Ch. Flair Peg O' My Heart

1973   Ch. Reveille's Reflection of Sheldon

ASSA Specialty Winners 1974–1989

1974   Ch. Halstors Peter Pumpkin, ROM (D)

1975   Ch. Sundowner Mr. Bojangles, CD/ROM (D)

1976   Benayr Chimera Colloquy (B)*

1977   Ch. Banchory Back Stop, ROM (D)

1978   Ch. Chenterra Thunderation, ROM (D)

1979   Ch. Chenterra Thunderation, ROM (D)

1980   Ch. Westwood Tuf Stuff of Coally (D)

1981   Ch. Kismet's Status Quo (D)

1982   (Ch.) Banchory Formal Notice, ROM (D)**

1983   Ch. Lynnlea Forever Amber, CD (B)

1984   Ch. Rorralore-Sportin' Chance, CD/ROM (D)

1985   Ch. MacDega One Day At A Time (B)

1986   Ch. Birch Hollow The Choir Boy (D)

1987   Ch. Chelsea Lynmark Love Affair (B)

1988   Ch. Lanbur Garden Party (B)

1989   Ch. Lakehill King O'The Road (D)

1990   Ch. Cameo Nick In Time

*since finished championship

**Win cancelled by AKC, and although dog is a champion, AKC has never published the title because of the suspension of the breeder's privileges.

13

The Shetland Sheepdog
Futurity Stakes

$\mathbf{A}$ FUTURITY is a special event that has been copied after those given at horse races. It is essentially an event for breeders. In the case of horses, the race is for two-year-olds. In dog events it is usually for puppies. However, national breed governing bodies make up their own rules. And some futurities, particularly for field dogs, cover dogs up to eighteen months of age.

About 1957 the American Shetland Sheepdog Association altered its futurity rules. These have remained essentially the same ever since. So, in this chapter, we report on the victors beginning with 1958.

Before giving the rules, let us try to report in as simple a fashion as possible what a futurity really is. A bitch is bred and high hopes are expected for the litter. So, before the pups are born, she is nominated and a small fee is paid.

At some period after the litter is whelped, a second fee is paid. This fee is for each individual puppy. For example, let us say that four puppies still look promising. Then the additional fee would be paid on all four. But if only one turns out well, then only it would be nominated.

Still a third fee would be paid at a future date, usually when the puppy is six months old. Then it would have to be nominated under its registered name. In addition, there is the entry fee for the show; usually, this is paid to the specialty show, less the superintendent's handling charges. All the money that has come in through the futurity nominations themselves is paid out to the winners. There are usually special cash awards that go to breeder and to the owner of the sire.

The rules that govern the American Shetland Sheepdog Association futurity follow: The futurity is open to all members of the association. Futurity classes are judged in advance of the regular classes at the specialty show. Dogs entered in the futurity must also be entered in the regular breed classes at the show.

There are two classes, six to nine months, and nine to twelve months of age. The two puppy winners then compete for best in the futurity. Nominations of bitches must be made before the puppies are whelped. And puppies eligible for competition must be born within a year to six months before the futurity show date. The nomination fee for the bitch is paid when her name is submitted.

Ten weeks after the date of birth, a second payment must be made, and the puppy's sire, dam and sex must be given. Then at six months of age, a final payment must be made, and the puppy's name, sex and color must be given. Fee amounts are set by the ASSA.

Nomination fees for six to nine months competition are used for that class, and fees for nine to twelve months competition are used for that class. Prize money is divided as follows: First, 40 percent; second, 30 percent; third, 20 percent and fourth, 10 percent. Special money prizes are given by the American Shetland Sheepdog Association to the breeder of the best in the futurity, and to the owner of the sire.

These are the basic rules for the futurity. A full set of rules and entry blanks can be obtained from the American Shetland Sheepdog Association itself. Officers of the club change from time to time. But since the association is a member of the American Kennel Club, the address of the secretary can be obtained from it. However, those wanting to enter the futurity must join the ASSA itself to become eligible.

Perhaps here it should be pointed out that since a futurity is a nonregular part of a dog show, the judge does not have to be licensed by the American Kennel Club. Often a noted breeder will be asked to officiate. Sometimes breed specialists will be asked to judge the regular classes, and multiple- or all-breed judges will preside over the futurity.

Here are the winners, judges and owners, starting with the inception of the new rules:

Year	Judge	Dog	Owner
1958	A. R. Miller	Fascination O'Page's Hill	Page's Hill Kennels
1959	Louis Murr	Grayson's Bright Minx	W. and E. Brady
1960	Mrs. W. H. Gray	Kiloren Toby of Pocono	Mrs. Walter Ford
1961	Alex Gibbs	Fast Brook O'Pages Hill	Page's Hill Kennels
1962	Mrs. H. W. Nichols, Jr.	Ch. Gra-John's Little G-Man	Gra-John Kennels
1963	Mrs. James Hausman	Goodhill Blue Mist	Mrs. J. Gooding

Ch. Benayr Hot Wheels, owned by Michael and Lyn Reese, has won five Specialty Bests.   *Rockwell*

Ch. Brangay the Name of the Game, owned by Annette and Richard Burchell and handled in the ring by Mrs. Burchell.
          Lindemaier

Ch. Rockwood's Gold Strike, owned, bred and handled by Barbara Kenealy, was chosen first in the Herding Group at the 1988 Westminster KC show.

Ch. Cee Bar Blue on Blue with Nancy Howard. *Mikron*

1964	Alva Rosenberg	King Hector O'Page's Hill	Page's Hill Kennels
1965	M. T. L. Downing	Gra-John's Mollie Bea	Gra-John Kennels
1966	Robert Reedy	Storm Signal O'Page's Hill	Page's Hill Kennels
1967	Constance Hubbard	Tiree Hall Merry Marquis	S. and H. Hendrickson
1968	Mary Van Wagenen	Merri Lon Night Shadows	D. and Vernon Peterson
1969	Mrs. Lloyd Johnson	Scotchguard The Admiral	A. and D. Towne
1970	Mrs. Helen Hendrickson	Beltane The Buccaneer	P. and B. Curry
1971	Laura Sawin	Tentagel The Folk-Singer	D. Reeves and R. Fletcher
1972	Mrs. Kitty Reconnu	Betit's Mr. Louisiana	Betty Impastato and Sharlene DeFee

Futurity Winners 1974–1990

1973   Barwood's Rhapsody (own: Barbara Thompson and Robert White)

1974   Lingard Something Special (own: Jeu and Lemerand)

1975   MacDega Sergeant Pepper* (own: T. Coen and Barger)

1976   Benayr Sam I Am (own: B. and S. Bentley)

1977   Pixie Dell Dawn's Early Light (own: Shirrell and Miller)

1978   Stonewall Nina Ricci (own: E. Sanchez)

1979   MacDega Barwood Birthright* (own: T. Coen)

1980   Windhover Dawns Early Light* (own: A. and T. Power)

1981   Wildoak Moon Reflection* (own: M. and P. Character)

1982   MacDega Marrakech* (own: T. and N. Coen)

1983   Whitegates Anything U Can Do* (own: J. and T. Pavey)

1984   Shaldan's Pineland Checkmate* (own: B. Gurak)

1985   Tall Timber Silver Gi Gosh (own: N. Bosse)

1986   Cameo The Good Bi Girl* (own: M. Marlow)

1987   MacDega Sultana* (own: T. and N. Coen)

1988   Zion's Bright Signature (own: S. and S. Vicchito)

1989   Cabriole's Tender Mercy (own: F. Gold)

1990   Ch. Sharokee Finer Things (own: Sandra Mathiesen and Sharon Mausy)

* have since won championships

Am., Can. Ch. Brow
Acres Bette. *Robe*

Can. Ch. Wee Bonnie Blue Lass, An
Can. CD, owned by Bonnie Lafferty.

14

Canadian Beginnings

THE CULT of the Shetland Sheepdog began later in Canada than it did in the United States. It is not known when the first Shelties arrived. The first to be registered, in 1930, were owned by Miss Sybil Fincham of Montreal. Miss Fincham was an importer who bought and imported dogs of a dozen breeds, and in astonishing numbers. The Canadian Kennel Club took punitive action against her, but not before she had made a lasting impression on several breeds, and particularly on the Shetland Sheepdog.

Her first import was Queen of Mountfort, a daughter of Specks of Mountfort, which arrived in Canada in April 1930. Several weeks later, Wizbang Godiva and Wizbang Magnus came. On May 27, 1930, a large consignment of dogs arrived for Miss Fincham. There were Nan of Mountfort with her progeny, littermates Sable Jock and Sable Naneen; Wizbang Luxury; and Eng. Ch. Specks of Mountfort. The same consignment included a Wire-haired Fox Terrier and an English Setter.

The next year seven dogs were registered, all by Miss Fincham. These were Callah Mohr, Can. Ch. Marbles of Greyhill, a blue merle Ros Mairl, Roseberry and three littermates sired by Eng. Ch. Gawaine of Cameliard. They were Wizbang Fairy Queen, Wizbang Gold Gawaine and Wizbang Joy. Their dam was Wizbang Godiva and, as the saying goes, they were imported "in utero." If Wizbang Joy can be said to have been bred in Canada, since she was born there, then she can be called the first Canadian-bred champion.

Actually, the first Canadian Shetland Sheepdog champion of record was Eltham Park Anahassitt. Mrs. William F. Dreer had shown the dog in Canada in 1929. In 1930 Mrs. Harkness Edwards took the dog back to Canada to complete its championship. Mrs. Dreer also exhibited Wee Laird O'Downfield in Canada, but he did not complete his championship.

The rules for registration and for the granting of championships were less stringent in Canada then than they are now. This was also true to some extent with the American Kennel Club. Thus, a dog with a slightly defective pedigree, or none, might have won a championship. It could not be registered, but if bred to a registered dog, the offspring would be eligible for registration. In those days, a dog registered by the American Kennel Club could win a championship without going through the formality of being registered by the Canadian Kennel Club. Today, the Canadian Kennel Club will not issue a championship certificate until the dog has been registered with it.

Wizbang and Marbles of Greyhill won championships in 1931. The following year, two unregistered dogs, Dixie and Patch, won championships. Owned by Mrs. W. G. Clark, they won at shows in the Vancouver, British Columbia, area. They were bred by G. B. Caird of the English-registered Chestnut affix after he moved to Vancouver, but they were not CKC registered.

James D. Strachan is one of the immortals of Canadian dogdom. He served as an officer of the Canadian Kennel Club for at least twenty-two years. Strachan was already well known as a Collie breeder when he became attracted to the Shetland Sheepdog. His first Sheltie was Nattie Gallagher O'Pages Hill, which he bought from William W. Gallagher.

In 1933 Nattie Gallagher won her championship. Gallagher himself campaigned Piccolo O'Pages Hill to a Canadian title that year. Also winning championships in 1933 were Ch. Sable Naneen, owned by Miss E. E. Sparrow, and Ch. Tiny Betty of Walnut Hall, owned by Miss Katherine H. Edwards. These two American dogs won at Oakville, National Kennel Club, Toronto Ladies Kennel Association and Guelph.

Eltham Park Anahassitt, Piccolo O'Pages Hill and Tiny Betty of Walnut Hall were never registered with the Canadian Kennel Club. They returned to the United States. Their only direct influence upon the breed comes from the attraction they drew from Canadian breeders. However, since Canadian and American breeders have crossbred their stock, all three can be found far back in Canadian as well as in American pedigrees.

One of the greatest of the early Canadian breeders was William Henderson of Toronto. He established the Alford Kennels. Henderson had bought Ch. Wizbang Joy and Wizbang Godiva from Miss Fincham. Ch. Wizbang Joy, a great producer, was the dam of champions Alford Achievement, Alford Clansman, Alford Heatherbelle and Alford Guinea Gold. Wizbang Godiva produced Ch. Alford Champagne Bubble. Henderson also imported Lord Lovell O'Pages Hill from Gallagher, and he bred Kingsvale Lad. Both became champions.

James Strachan's Coltness Kennels appears in the champions' lists in both the United States and Canada. Among his better-known champions was Coltness Little Lizbeth. He also owned Ch. Pocono Pimpernel, which he bought from Dorothy A. Foster of Austel, Georgia. This dog combined the bloodlines of two great American foundation kennels. These were Elizabeth D. Whelen's Pocono

Ch. Hi-Hope's Merry Imp, UD, Am. CDX, was also the dam of two champions.

Allen

Can., Am. Ch. Hi-Hope's Echo O'Imp, a memorable winner.   *Powell*

Ch. Sunnycrest Black Topper, owned by Mr. and Mrs. R. C. Kress.

Ch. Kel-Lani's Claire de Lune.

Left to Right: Ch. Terian's Aire Fare, owned by Deanna Roche; Ch. Pattoo's Song of Holly and Ch. Allmac's Le Centenaire, CD, owned by Joan Wiik.

Kennels and Mrs. Foster's Timberidge Kennels. Strachan also owned Ch. Alford Champagne Bubble.

However great his dogs, and however broad his breeding program, Strachan's greatest contribution to the breed came through his prestige. He was the secretary-treasurer of the Canadian Kennel Club, and he was among the leaders of the Collie fraternity on both sides of the border. When the great Collie breeder turned to the Sheltie, people everywhere became interested in it.

The breed spread quickly across Canada. MacKenzie Matheson of Caulfield, British Columbia, founded his Caulfield Kennels, and the Caulfield name quickly became famous on both sides of the border. Matheson bought Black Sachem O'Pages Hill from Gallagher, and the dog easily became a champion. Two of Matheson's other foundation dogs were Ch. Caulfield Little Joker and Can. Ch. Caulfield Silver Lady.

These, then, were the pioneers of Sheltie-dom in Canada. They imported top dogs from England, and they freely used the best of the early American dogs. And in doing so, they laid a solid foundation for the healthy growth of the breed in Canada.

Can. Ch. Arpeggio Timerider O'Forever, owned by Mr. and Mrs. Glenn Roadhouse, is a BIS winner. *Lindt*

Ch. Forever Arpeggio Brett Butler, Canada's top-winning Sheltie in history, is owned by Leslie Rogers and Donna Roadhouse. His record includes 188 BBs under one hundred judges as well as seventy-nine Group firsts from an international array of judges. *Lindt*

15

Modern Shelties in Canada

CANADIAN Shetland Sheepdog breeders and owners have unfortunately—and unfairly—been forced to live under the shadow of their American counterparts. There has been a general lack of familiarity on the part of the Americans with Canadian dogs. And there has been a tendency to downgrade the Canadian dogs.

Yet the border between the two countries has not been an iron curtain. Dogs have crossed the border both ways, both for show and for breeding purposes. There are many dogs that are Canadian and American champions. Yet the general unfamiliarity of Americans with Canadian successes is great. And because of it, we are departing from the general format of this book to give the records of some of the older Canadian kennels. They indicate how the Canadian lines have been established, and they also prove the points made above.

Basically, the Canadians have achieved greatest success by linebreeding to the lines that produced Ch. Timberidge Temptation and Ch. Prince George O'Pages Hill. One of the fine kennels, Ronas Hill, based its program on Alford dogs (see the previous chapter), also Pocono, and then Helensdale. Pocono and Badgerton often appear in Canadian pedigrees.

Ch. Coltness Commander was the first Canadian-bred dog to win an American championship. He was a son of Ch. Nattie Gallagher O'Pages Hill who was sent back to the United States to be bred to Ch. Mowgli. He is proof of the points made above.

In the following analysis of kennels, we are presenting five not so much in the order of their successes as in the order of their founding. It has been observed that the average life of people in the dog game is five years. But with Shetland Sheepdogs, this has not been true, either in Canada or the United States. Many of the great kennels, founded forty-odd years ago, are still both active and successful.

Ronas Hill Kennels of Mrs. E. F. Lovett of Stittsville, Ontario, was founded in December 1949. The foundation dogs were Ch. Alford Laddie of Glenleigh, Ch. Alford Ballerina (a half sister) and Aylmer Chorine. Chorine produced five champions, including two American champions. It is worthy of note that these latter two dogs—American and Canadian Ch. Dixie Belle of Ronas Hill and American Ch. Orange Flare of Ronas Hill—produced American champions for Hampshire Kennels in the United States.

Another Ronas Hill foundation bitch was American and Canadian Ch. Pocono Trinket of Windy Oaks. Trinket was a remarkable dog. She was shown at an American Shetland Sheepdog Association national specialty show in the veterans class. She was sixteen and one half years old at the time, and she won an ovation.

In 1953 Ronas Hill imported English Ch. Helensdale Wendy from James Saunders of Scotland. She was a great producer. And so it can be seen that Helensdale has played an important part in Canada just as it has in the United States.

E. H. and Frances Clark established their Hi-Hope Kennels at Richmond, British Columbia, in 1954. Their first champion was Hi-Hope's Merry Imp. She won a Utility Dog title in Canada and a Companion Dog Excellent title in the United States. To the best of the writer's knowledge, she is the only Shetland Sheepdog in North American history to win an all-breed Best in Show and a UD degree.

This kennel purchased and imported Timberidge Typesetter. He became a Canadian champion and won his major points in the United States. A son of this dog, out of Merry Imp, was Ch. Hi-Hope's Echo O'Imp. He, too, was a Best in Show winner. When bred to Badgerton Vain Vanessa, he sired a litter of five champions, two of which won American championships as well. Again, the high quality of the Canadian dogs is proven.

Badgertown Vain Vanessa also produced four champions when bred to Ch. Timberidge Typesetter. One of these, Ch. Hi-Hope's Badgertown Canadienne, has been a producer for Badgerton Kennels in the United States. Kinswood bloodlines also appear in Hi-Hope pedigrees.

The Terian Kennels of Joan Wiik of Saskatoon, Saskatchewan, were founded in late 1958. Saskatoon is not well located for making either great production or show records. Yet Terian has one of the best records in Canada.

Mrs. Wiik won her first championship with Terian's April Lass, CD, a daughter of Ch. Timberidge Typesetter, CD. She added to her kennels Ch. Saravan's Elegant Lad, of Thistlerose breeding, and later, Ch. Kawartha's Fair Game. The Terian record also includes a Best in Show winner—Ch. Terian's Tuesday Wendy.

Can. Ch. Miquelon Bootblack, owned by Doug and Gwen Perrin and bred by Joyce Wastle and Denise Cornelssen.

Can., Am. Ch. Trevannes Any Day Now, owned by Jack and Colleen Andrus.

Another great kennel founded in the late 1950s is Kel-Lani. Its foundation dogs were Ch. Starcross Wonder Boy, CDX, and Sweet Leilani of Lorel, CD. They bred an offspring of those two to Ch. Geronimo Son Rey, CD, a champion in the United States, Canada and Mexico. From that mating came Ch. Kel-Lani's Moonglow, CD, dam of five champions. The kennel was founded by Mrs. D. O'Dare, Miss Chris O'Dare and J. Horton.

It is not possible to analyze all the great Canadian kennels here, though their records will appear later. However, as a measure of Canadian and American cooperation, we do give here the Meridian Kennels of Mrs. Hazel Slaughter, Bois des Filion, Quebec. To mention it, however, we must also mention Summit Kennels, formerly of Quebec, but now in the United States. The two kennels have continued their cooperation, even though now so widely separated.

Meridian Kennels was founded basically on Ronas Hill stock. Hazel Slaughter, under the Meridian name, has bred nineteen champions. Her American and Canadian Ch. Meridian's Miss Behave was the top-winning Sheltie in Canada in 1968, and the dam of Ch. Summit's Gay Nineties, the second top winner in 1970. Miss Behave is the dam of six champions, and her daughter, Ch. Summit's Gay Abandon, of eight.

Ch. Summit's Gold Dust, CD, is by Ch. Nashcrest Golden Note out of Ch. Cinderella's Gypsy of Ronas Hill. He has sired twelve champions, and some of his progeny have been excellent sires and producers on both sides of the border.

Most of these Canadian breeders have paid particular attention to temperament and character. A number of the abovementioned dogs have won obedience titles.

CANADIAN STATISTICS

Canadian Shetland Sheepdog fanciers are blessed by having one of the world's greatest authorities on the breed as their historian and statistician. He is Leslie B. Rogers of Langley, British Columbia. Mr. Rogers is a librarian by profession. But he has bred and owned Collies, Borzois and Scottish Deerhounds, as well as his beloved Shetland Sheepdogs. He is also currently breeding and showing Pomeranians. He has judged all over the United States, Canada, Australia and New Zealand.

He began breeding Shelties in 1960, and his record has been remarkable. It includes three all-breed Best in Show winners. These are Ch. Forever Silk Tassel, Ch. Arpeggio Timerider O'Forever and Ch. Forever Arpeggio Brett Butler. All three were "Number One" in their years.

Mr. Rogers's dogs have won fourteen Bests in Show in all-breed competition, including ten in one year. He now shares a partnership with Donna Roadhouse of Arpeggio Shelties. She also helps with statistical work.

Mr. Rogers has divided his statistics into the following categories: Best in Show Winners, Sires, Dams, Statistical Comments. The first Shetland Sheepdog to win a truly major award was Ch. Alford Heatherbelle. She won a best Canadian-bred in an all-breed show. This award is no longer given.

The Best in Show Winners

Some 110 Shetland Sheepdogs have won the coveted title of Best in Show. The first to do so was Ch. Tayside Bonnie Prince, nearly thirty-five years ago. The first female to win a best in show was Ch. Hi-Hope's Merry Imp, UD. This dog was bred, owned and shown by Frances Clark, who still carries on. Merry Imp won from the classes under the late American judge Chris Shuttleworth.

The great winners are listed below. Their country of origin is listed following their names.

14 Bests   Ch. Forever Arpeggio Brett Butler (Can.)

9 Bests   Ch. Banchory Key Witness (U.S.)

6 Bests   Ch. Winsawn's First Choice, CDX (U.S.)

5 Bests   Ch. Mantoga's Bobby Shaftoe (Can.)

5 Bests   Ch. Genson's Intrepid Man (Can.)

4 Bests   Simaril's Tarna's Theme (Can., female)

3 Bests   Ch. Delamantha's Desiderata (Can., female)
              Ch. Banchory Backstop (U.S.)
              Ch. Alert Thistle Lass (Can., female)
              Ch. Is Charles Rex O'Satelier (Can.)
              Ch. Sheldon Raspberry Ruffle (Can., female)
              Ch. Sundial Rendezvous (U.S.)
              Ch. Terian's Aire Fare (Can.)

2 Bests   Ch. Sir Joshua Of Winslow (U.S.)
              Ch. Banchory Eye Of The Storm (U.S.)

Here are some firsts for the breed:

First sable and white male: Ch. Tayside Bonnie Prince (Can.)
First sable and white female: Ch. Hi-Hope's Merry Imp, UD (Can.)
First tri-color male: Ch. Richmore Roustabout (U.S.)
First tri-color female: Ch. Cloverleaf's Tri-Jet (Can.)
First blue merle male: Ch. Roydon's Indigo of Brookbend (U.S.)
First blue merle female: Ch. Timberlawn Blue Haze O'Forelyn (U.S.)
First multiple Best in Show winners: Ch. Terian's Aire Fare (Can., male)
      Ch. Delamantha's Desiderata (Can., female)

Leading Shetland Sheepdog Sires

Am. & Can. Ch. Reveille's Reflection of Sheldon (Can.) at the time of writing had sired fifty champions. He was owned and handled by Doreen and William Randall of Sheldon Shelties of Ontario. He became an all-breed Best in Show winner as a puppy. In 1973 he was owner-handled to Best of Breed at the American Shetland Sheepdog Association National Specialty, judged by Charlotte Clem McGowan of Rorralore Shelties.

Am. Ch. Halstor's Peter Pumpkin (U.S.), although he never appeared in a Canadian show, has sired some forty-odd Canadian champions, and appears in the pedigree background of many kennels. He was owned and shown by Tom Coen of MacDega Shelties. He was a multiple Best in Show winner himself, and won the National American Specialty Show. In the United States he has sired more than 150 champions, a record probably not equaled by any other dog in any breed. He was in Japan for a time, and sired champions in that country as well.

Sires of More Than Twenty-five Canadian Champions

Ch. Esquire's Casino Royale (U.S.), a sable and white son of Ch. Halstor's Peter Pumpkin, was owned and handled by Joseph C. Brant of Sateilier Kennels of British Columbia. He sired specialty winners as well as Best in Show winners.

Am. & Can. Ch. Banchory Formal Notice (U.S.) was owned and handled by Clare and Donna Harden of Banchory Shelties of Portland, Oregon. He was not used past five years of age. He sired multiple champions of all colors.

Am. & Can. Ch. Banchory Backstop (U.S.), a tri-color, was owned by Irene and Bud Dishi of Akirene Shelties in British Columbia. He was an all-breed Best in Show winner in both Canada and the United States, and was a Best of Breed winner at the American Shetland Sheepdog Association National Specialty. He sired both all-breed and specialty-winning champions.

Sires of Twenty or More Champions

Ch. Boydlyn's Andy Devine, CD (U.S.)
Ch. Delamantha's Daybreak (Can.)
Ch. Sunnybrook Heritage Spirit (U.S.), also a leading American sire

Sires of Fifteen or More Champions

Ch. Banchory Birthright, CDX (U.S.)
Ch. Banchory Count Down (U.S.)
Ch. Banchory High Born (U.S.)
Ch. Cherden Sock It To Em (U.S.)
Ch. Francehill Indigo, UD (U.K.)
Ch. Gray Dawn Reveille of Sea Isle (U.S.)
Ch. Rorralore Winter Sport (U.S.)
Ch. Sheldon Banner Boy (Can.)
Ch. Sheldon Korshelt Classic Look (Can.)
Ch. Sovereign Pumpkin of Astolat (U.S.)
Ch. Sovereign Ring's Legacy (Can.)
Ch. Teaberry Lane Ford of The Ring (U.S.)
Ch. Terian's Aire Fare (Can.)
Ch. Timberidge Typesetter, CD (U.S.)
Ch. Willow Acres Golden Rocket (Can.)

Can. Ch., OTCH Clan Lasslyn Carry the Day, Am. CDX, owned by Nancy Tyler.

Can. Ch. Forever Silk Tassel, a BIS winner owned by Donna Roadhouse, demonstrates the effortless, elastic gait that is essential to a correct Shetland Sheepdog.   *Hall*

Can. Ch. Patoo's Birth of the Blues, CD, is owned by Patricia Ristau and shown here with handler Denise Cornelssen.
Wainwright

Can. Ch. Madselin Dream Scape, a Specialty winner, shown here with owner Susan Carbert.

Ch. Banchory Counter Force (U.S.)
Ch. Banchory Deep Purple (U.S.)
Ch. Banchory Key Witness (U.S.)
Banchory Reflection (U.S.)
Ch. Banchory Showman of Shaylin (U.S.)
Ch. Bronze of Mantoga, UD (Can.)
Ch. Chenterra Thunderation (U.S.)
Delamantha Desideratason (Can.)
Ch. Gallantry Solid Success (Can.)
Ch. Honeyboy of Callart (U.K.)
Ch. Kel-Lani's Moonshine (Can.)
Ch. MacDega Mainstay (U.S.)
Ch. MacDega Mastery (U.S.)
Ch. MacDega The Piano Man (U.S.)
Ch. Miskela Darth Vader (Can.)
Ch. Quilcheena Blue Legend of Hi-Hope (Can.)
Ch. Ridgeside Star Wars (U.S.)
Ch. Romayne's Spartan Life (U.S.)
Ch. Rorralore Fair Prince (U.S.)
Ch. Shadland Midnight Classic (Can.)
Ch. Sheldon This Is The General (Can.)
Ch. Summit's Gold Dust, CD (Can.)
Ch. Sunnycrest Black Topper (Can.)
Ch. Sunura Drift On Misty Glen, UD (U.S.)

It is important to note the tremendous influence the Sea Isle Shelties of Mary Van Wagenen and Evelyn Davis have had on the breed. Many of the leading sires and dams trace their lineage to basic Sea Isle background. This is especially notable in the sable colors.

The influence of the Banchory Kennels of Clare and Donna Harden of Oregon and California has been phenomenal. This has been especially true in blue merles, tri-colors and bi-colors in both the United States and Canada.

Pedigree analysis of champions and champion producers pinpoint the source of success. A true breed enthusiast is a pedigree analyst who wants to know just where quality and characteristics originate.

Leading Canadian Dams

It is a rare honor to have a top-producing dam. Their opportunities to become leading producers are so much less than those of the males. Please note the number of these females who are also champions as well. That takes time and effort as well as giving an indication of individual quality.

Ch. Summit's Gay Abandon (U.S. & Can.), a sable and white, heads the list as the top-producing Sheltie female, having produced thirteen champions. Of a Sea Isle lineage, she thus far remains unchallenged as the leading producer. She was owned by the partnership of Hazel Slaughter (Canada) and Ruth Lane (U.S.).

Ch. Hausenbrook's Mischief Maker (Can.), a sable and white dam, produced ten champions, a wonderful accomplishment for two Canadian kennels—Sheldon and Genson Shelties, which both featured this dog in their breeding programs.

Ch. Blundell's Peg O'My Heart (Can.), a sable and white, produced nine champions for Shiralee Shelties, owned by Karen Zimmerman and her family. She was a daughter of a leading producer.

Badgerton Vain Vanessa (U.S.) was also the dam of nine champions, including several which made their American championships. Vanessa was owned by Frances Clark of Hi-Hope Kennels. Her progeny were also noted for their abilities in the obedience ring.

Dams of Seven or More Champions

Aylmer Chorine (Can.)
Ch. Cloverleaf's County Charm (Can.)
Ch. Kinggate Candle In The Rain (Can.)
Ch. Lauxly's Midnight Madness (Can.)
Ch. Whitegate's Lo And Behold (Can.)

Dams of Six or More Champions

Alford Jay Jay's Lassie (Can.)
Ch. Meridian's Miss Behave (Can.), dam of the No. 1 producer
Ch. Satelier's Mocha Sunrise, UD (Can.)
Ch. Sunnydell Love Story (U.S.)
Ch. Willowacres Golden Charm, CA (Can.)

Dams of Five or More Champions

Ch. Alfenlock Brooke Shields (Can.)
Ch. Chicwin Promised Victory (Can.)
Ch. Cinderella Gypsy Of Ronas Hill, UDT (Can.)
Ch. Clan Lasslyn Carryon (Can.)
Delamantha's Dove (Can.)
Ch. Dilharne Fortune (U.K.)
Doron's Taffy Ann (Can.)
Ch. Helensdale Wendy (U.K.)
Ch. Hi-Hope's Bonnie Naiad (Can.)
Ch. Keldabista's Special Edition (Can.)
Kel-Lani's Autumn Blaze (Can.)
Ch. Kel-Lani's Moonglow, CD (Can.)
Ch. Lucky Charm of Mantoga (Can.)
Ch. Minonamee Eugenie (Can.)
Satelier's Blessed Event (Can.)

Ch. Satelier's Rosemary (Can.)
Sunnycrest Mary Imp (Can.)
Ch. Tremur's Autumn Glory (Can.)
Whitegates On A Clear Day (Can.)
Whitegates Vanity Fair (Can.)

CANADIAN SHETLAND SHEEPDOG ASSOCIATION

In 1988, a national association for Shetland Sheepdogs came into being largely through the efforts of Joyce Wastle and Denise Cornelssen of Miquelon Shelties. It is partially modeled on the American Shetland Sheepdog Association. It is to be hoped that the Canadian Association will be able to hold a national specialty show annually. The show would, of course, be moved about the country to give all breeders and exhibitors a chance to enter.

The first breed booster show was held in Alberta and drew sixty-six entries, including seventeen champions. The judge was Dr. William Houpt of California. The breed winner was Ch. Forever Arpeggio Brett Butler, who then went on to win the herding group at the all-breed show.

The first president of the newly formed CSSA was Fred Baxtrome (Maracaibo Shelties) of St. Johns, Newfoundland. The membership is healthy in numbers and represents a cross-section of Sheltie fanciers throughout Canada. Its future looks promising.

Ch. Sharval the Delinquent established the British record of fifteen challenge certificates for Shetland Sheepdogs when he won BB at Crufts in 1972. Some twenty years later that record still stands.   *C. M. Cooke & Son*

16

Modern Shelties
in England and
New Zealand

ONE DOG that should be mentioned here is Ch. Sharval The Delinquent. He won fifteen challenge certificates, and also won Best of Breed at Crufts in 1972. He was black and white. His record had not been equaled before, and still stands. But for Americans, one line stands above the rest. It is called "C. H. E."

It is of great importance to Americans because of the influence its famous dogs had upon American bloodlines. Its great sires included Ch. Gawaine of Cameliard, Chestnut Rainbow, Ch. Uam Var of Houghton Hill and Ch. Nutkin of Houghton Hill. Nutkin came to America and can be found in many pedigrees.

English Kennel Club registrations for 1987 and 1988 show that the Sheltie stands fourteenth among the first twenty breeds, and just below Collies. Thus, in 1987, Shelties registered 3,048 and Collies, 4,259; in 1988 Shelties 2,751 and Collies 3,579. The Collie figures are for Rough Collies only.

New Zealand is a long way from most areas that raise and import or export dogs. It is true that New Zealand does produce great horses, which are then shipped to Australia. And New Zealanders are exporters of lamb and wool. As for purebred dogs, they can import from Australia and Tasmania, and of course from Great Britain.

Show dogs can be photogenic outside the breed ring, too. This charming study shows Ch. Simaril Tarna's Theme with her puppies Satinlace Pride of Simaril (left) and Simaril Man About Town.

Lindt

17

Shetland Sheepdog Litters

IN 1910 JAMES A. LOGGIE wrote an article on the Sheltie for Sydney Turner's *Kennel Encyclopedia*. In it, he wrote: "They are not prolific, having generally litters of about three or four; strange to say, females invariably predominate, being generally two to one." One cannot help wondering if this is true today. The Shetland Sheepdog has been bred worldwide for more than fifty years. Also, Shetland Islanders told the author that their sheep, cattle, ponies and dogs tended to lose their native characteristics when bred away from the islands.

The American Kennel Club records litters. Periodically, since 1953, the author has made litter studies at the American Kennel Club. Among other things, a record is made at the AKC of the largest litters ever whelped in each breed. The records are based upon the number of puppies living at the time application is made to register the litter. A bitch might, for instance, whelp twenty puppies. However, fifteen might die within the first few days after birth. The litter would then be registered as one of five.

Let us suppose that the breed record is a litter of sixteen. If an application comes in listing a litter of seventeen, the American Kennel Club will investigate to be certain that the litter actually is one of seventeen as claimed. If found to be true, then a new breed mark is made. The largest litter ever whelped is said to have been twenty-three puppies, born to a Foxhound. However, no effort was ever made to register the litter. American Kennel Club officials believe the puppies came from three litters whelped on the same day.

At the time of the author's first study in 1953, the largest recorded litter of

Can. Ch. Carmylie The Merry Chase, CD, owned by Jean Simmonds, is a Herding Group winner. *Ashbey*

Am., Can. Ch. Winsawn's First Choice, Am. UD, TT, Can. CDX, owned and handled by Kathy Murphy, is an all-breed BIS and Specialty winner in the U.S. and Canada. *Mikron*

Am., Can. Ch. Rosewood's Christy the Clown, a multiple BIS winner, bred, owned and handled to her good record by Rosemary Petter.

Shetland Sheepdog puppies was one of eight. A few years later, Mrs. Alane L. Lubker (now Gomez) reported a litter of ten with nine survivors litter-registered by the AKC. But litters of nine or ten are very rare. Only two litters out of 731 had as many as nine or ten puppies.

This data was taken from computer records that listed litters in brackets of 1–2, 3–4, and on to 21–22 and 22 plus. If memory serves correctly, the twenty-two figure belongs to a St. Bernard. All twenty-two puppies were living at the time the AKC received the application, but more than half had died by the time an AKC field officer investigated. We cannot say for certain, because of the above bracketing, whether the two Sheltie litters were of nine or ten puppies, or one of nine and one of ten. The data do show that 292 of the 731 litters had either three or four puppies. That is a percentage of 39.9. The 5–6 bracket had 33.5 percent or 245 litters. And the 1–2 bracket had 19.2 percent or 141 litters. Of the balance, fifty-one litters, or 6.9 percent, had seven or eight puppies, and the two litters in the 9–10 bracket represented only 0.2 percent.

A. Hamilton Rowan, Jr., secretary of the American Kennel Club, then personally helped the writer in a random study of 105 litters. In this case, we were more interested in the ratio of males to females than in actual litter size. There were 206 bitch puppies and only 135 males. Thus, Loggie's ratio of two to one no longer holds. But females do enjoy a strong lead over males. In seventeen of the litters there were no males among the forty puppies. There were seven all-male litters totaling fifteen puppies. It will be seen from this that when only one sex is present in the litter, that litter is usually small. When there are large one-sex litters, they are usually female. There were three litters of five bitches each.

It can be said that, in general, the largest dogs have the largest litters, and the smallest dogs have the smallest litters. We mentioned the St. Bernard litter of twenty-two. A Great Dane had a litter of nineteen. At least forty-eight breeds have had litters of twelve or more. Collies have recorded many large litters, including one of sixteen. In a 1957 study, the author made a random breed check of 506 litters totaling 2,490 puppies. There were 1,301 males and 1,189 females.

Ch. Hundi Stamp of Approval, bred by Leilani Jaquez.

Ch. Barwood Cabriole Razor's Edge, owned by Barbara and Kenneth Linden and bred by Barbara Thompson and Fury Gold.

Am., Can. Ch. Whitegates Anything U Can Do, owned in Japan by Kiyoko Mukouda.

18

Genetics, Color and Coat in the Shetland Sheepdog

with Sue Ann Bowling

$\mathbf{M}$AMMALS as a group are among the most colorless of nature's creations. They cannot match the colors of the fish and reptiles. And they are hopelessly common when compared to the fantastic plumage and colors of the birds. Human beings and dogs are mammals. People, perhaps envying the reptiles and birds, have tattooed their bodies and painted their faces. They have stretched earlobes and lips, and have even altered the shapes of the breasts. Probably they first wore clothes more as ornamentation than as a protection from the weather.

Charles Darwin gave an example of this in his book *The Cruise of the Beagle*. The Beagle lay offshore of Tierra del Fuego. Curious natives came out in their canoes to see the ship and the strange white men. All were naked. Among them were women who were nursing newborn babies. Crew members gave them blankets. But the blankets were immediately torn into strips and distributed among the people to be used as decorations.

Perhaps you wonder how this preamble affects dogs. Dogs are said to be color-blind. Yet, if so, of what use is the remarkable range of coat color shown by purebred dogs? This question is asked because it is a general rule that animals use color as a means of identification. With the dog, a possible answer is that people, unable to develop color and plumage in themselves, have done so in dogs. People could, and did, develop exotic skin colors in the hairless dogs. And dogs were developed with wire coats, short coats, off-standing guard hairs and coats of astonishing length. Dogs were also developed that, like the Shetland Sheepdog, have an outer, harsher coat, and a softer, dense undercoat. And finally, some dogs were produced that, like the Maltese, have no undercoat at all.

Now if the dog is color-blind, it is not necessarily form blind. There is excellent evidence to indicate that dogs of a given breed can easily identify others of their breed. And evidence also exists to suggest that dogs have a sense of beauty as well as of form. Bitches, when in season, will seek a mate of their own breed. If they cannot reach such a male, then they tend to seek out certain males. Thus, a given mongrel may be the sire of half the dogs in a village. This evidence suggests that they recognize what is to them beauty of form. And the dogs that seem to them to be the most beautiful are those that have thick, heavy coats— specifically Shetland Sheepdogs, Collies and Chow Chows.

The climate of the Shetland Islands is about as inhospitable for a sheepdog as any in the world. We must believe that the islands' sheepdogs were, in 1900, well able to stand the climate. But the dogs of that day would be considered severely lacking in coat if brought into the modern show ring. Modern breeders have developed coats that probably would be more of a handicap than an aid to a working sheepdog in any climate. But the modern Sheltie coat satisfies the esthetic senses of both the breeders and their dogs.

Most mammalian color, whether of skin or of hair, in people or dogs is dependent upon a pigment named melanin. Melanin is said to be controlled by a gene. A given gene may express itself in various ways, and these expressions are called allelic genes or alleles. For example, when two genes are not identical, with one representing black hair and the other yellow, they are called alleles.

A dog's color is dependent upon the deposit of melanin in the pigment cells of the skin or hair. One set of allelic genes will control the deposit of melanin. But another set determines the actual color the melanin will be. The melanin will vary from black to mahogany red to pink. And the so-called yellow series of melanin will vary from tan and yellow to a whitish cream. Often the cream is so nearly absent as to make the dog appear to be almost wholly white, as in the Samoyed or West Highland White Terrier.

Lack of any melanin produces albinism. The albino is considered to be the result of a genetic error. It should be pointed out here that albinism is not limited to the hair and skin, but affects all the tissues of the body. True albinos are rare among dogs. The only ones ever observed by the author were three Pekingese puppies. As will be seen later, white or whitish Shetland sheepdogs sometimes do appear. But they are not albinos.

There are dogs whose color we call blue. But blue pigment is very rare in mammals and it is entirely absent in the hair of dogs. The author has researched world literature, and has studied the results of analyses of more than two hundred furs, but can find no mention of blue-pigmented hair. He has also queried research professors and geneticists. Blue pigment simply does not exist in dogs; but more about this later.

Shetland Sheepdogs have a wider range of color patterns than almost any

Ch. Springmist Troy O'Scotspride, owned by Loretta Willcuts.

Jan

Am., Can. Ch. Banchory Strike Me Silver, owned in Japan by Tetsuo Miyama.

other breed, Collies and the Arctic breeds excepted. These colors are black and white; black and tan; black, white and tan; sable (ranging from golden through mahogany) and white; and blue merle and white. There are, of course, prohibitions and penalties. Rustiness in a black or blue coat, washed out or degenerate colors (such as pale sable and faded blue), conspicuous white body spots, and with more than 50 percent white, are among the prohibitions. Sable merles bring severe penalties in some countries, and all bar brindles. The white, or whitish, dogs mentioned earlier are usually destroyed at birth, as explained later.

It is not our purpose to go into a detailed explanation of color inheritance in Shetland Sheepdogs. Indeed such an explanation is beyond all but those who have spent a lifetime studying the color genetics of dogs. Often these people do not agree. And few have made a thorough study of the Shetland Sheepdog. Those interested in this immensely complicated field are referred to four excellent texts:

> *Genetics of the Dog*, by Malcolm B Willis, Howell Book House, N.Y., 1989
>
> *The Inheritance of Coat Color in Dogs*, by C. C. Little, Howell Book House, N.Y., 1957
>
> *Inheritance in Dogs*, by O. Winge, Comstock Press, Ithaca, N.Y., 1950
>
> *Dog Breeding and Reproduction and Genetics*, by S. A. Asdell, Little, Brown, Boston, 1966

We will, however, report that information which Shetland Sheepdog breeders themselves have found. And we will include some additional information on the somewhat puzzling problems of the blue merle. Two tri-colors can produce golden sable. Two sables can produce black and white. Two blue merles can produce tri-colors. "It is that mixed up," as one Sheltie breeder put it. One reason is that the color alleles can be affected by others known as color intensity factors. For example, one of these can reduce ruddy-colored melanin to tan. And the same factor, or another, can reduce orange to golden or cream. One intensity factor can change a dark color to a gray, or even to a whitish shade. Still another can produce patches of black on a lighter ground color, with interruptions of white. This factor produces the harlequin in Great Danes, and possibly the blue merle of Collies and Shetland Sheepdogs.

In discussing color, one Collie breeder remarked to the author, "Blue merles are not blue, they are gray." But they are not the gray known to geneticists as agouti, nor are they a true gray of any kind. And neither are they a pigment blue. The blue color is an illusion. The reader will get a partial explanation of this in the chapter on eye color. But we might cite here a similar illusion that we sometimes see in the human face. Say that a man has a very black head of hair and a very heavy beard. When he is clean-shaven, his beard appears blue, and we sometimes speak of the blue beard.

An independent gene series determines that certain hairs will be black. An intense black melanin will be spread evenly through the hair. But a modifier, an allele known as the blue dilute, will affect other hairs. In these, the black pigments will be clumped and scattered, with larger or smaller spaces between them. Then we will have the blue effect known as Tyndall blue. Submicroscopic particles refract and reflect the blue and violet rays, thus creating the blue effect. The blue will be deeper or grayer according to the spacing of the clumps of pigment. The black melanin tends to absorb the light, while the submicroscopic particles in between diffuse, reflect and refract the blues and violets.

Recently, a Shetland Sheepdog breeder remarked that one of her blue merles sometimes appeared to be a lavender color. This could mean simply that more violet rays are being diffused than are pure blue rays. But we speak of blue and lavender sheens. The author has no authority for what follows, but it seems to me that some blue merles show iridescence. This is the quality of being able to change colors when reflecting light from various angles. Iridescence is caused by another factor known as interference. Whether or not it is actually a factor in creating the sheen in some blue merles remains to be studied. But in the light of our present knowledge, it should not be ignored.

Since possible Shetland Sheepdog colors can be so varied, and yet so pleasing, we can dismiss all of them here except the blue merle. The reason is that breeding for the blue merles can be dangerous, and even disastrous, unless the breeder understands the problems involved. For that reason, we go into the problem at some depth.

The color is said to have come into the Shetland Sheepdog through Collie crosses. Many such crosses were known in the early history of the breed. Yet J. A. Loggie's 1910 article, which we have quoted in full and was actually written in 1909, indicates that the blue merle was already an established breed color before any serious crosses to Collies were introduced.

The Shetland Sheepdog breed standard recognizes three colors: black, blue merle and sable, marked with varying amounts of white and/or tan. During the early days of the breed in the United States, and in fact until 1959, predominantly white dogs were also allowed. The colors and color genetics are similar to those in Collies, with three exceptions. The first is the fact that the Sheltie standard excludes the color-headed white, although they do occur in Shelties. The second is that black and white (and blue merle and white) without any tan markings has survived in Shelties. Finally, the relationship of sable to the black-pigmented colors is not quite as clear-cut in Shelties as seems to be the case in Collies.

In discussing the inheritance of these colors, it is important to recognize that, from a genetic point of view, there are at least three distinct sets of genes that combine to give the accepted colors in both Collies and Shelties. The first set controls the amount of tan pigment versus the amount of black, independent of the presence of white or merling. The second, merle, dilutes whatever black pigment is present in a somewhat patchy fashion and the third controls the white markings.

In the first group, sable (tan with a variable amount of black overlay) is normally dominant over black and tan (black with tan markings on the head, chest, legs and under the tail). In Shelties, both sable and black and tan in turn are dominant over black without tan. It is not yet clear whether the black without tan is a separate gene in the same series that produces sables and black/tans or the result of a recessive gene that suppresses tan points, and there are Sheltie breeders who will argue either way. What is clear is that black-to-black matings normally produce only black offspring, black to black and tan or both parents black and tan can produce black and tan and may produce black without tan, and a mating in which at least one parent is sable can produce all sables, sable and black/tan, sable and black, or all three colors. Black, of course, does not occur without tan in Collies, though black-and-white Border Collies are common enough. The black of Shelties, however, is clearly distinct from the black of Border Collies (or of most other breeds), which is dominant over sable.

The merle gene is present in most of the British and Australian herding breeds, as well as the dapple Dachshund and the harlequin Great Dane. When present in a single dose it dilutes portions of any black or liver pigment in the coat to blue-gray or to fawn with a grayish or even lavender cast. Eyes may also be partly diluted, and a merle may have one or both eyes entirely or partly blue. In Shelties and Collies, where liver is not an acceptable color, black becomes a blue-gray with black splotches, known as blue merle. If a sable is bred to a blue merle, some of the offspring may be sable merles. These as adults range from perfectly ordinary sable through sable with blue or partly blue eyes to some very strange colors indeed. (I have seen one that looked like a blue merle with a sable head.)

A merle-to-merle breeding can produce puppies with two doses of the merle gene. These puppies are usually handicapped to some extent, often being deaf, blind or lacking eyes entirely, and sometimes sterile. As they are not usually suitable as pets, the usual and safest breeding rule is to avoid producing them by breeding blue merles only to blacks with or without tan. (The major argument against breeding blue merles to sables is that sable merle offspring may be thought to be sables, and if two unsuspected sable merles are mated the result may be one or more defective white puppies). Now and then an experienced breeder will make a merle-to-merle breeding deliberately to help fix some other desired trait. White puppies from such matings are usually destroyed at birth, but in recent years several of otherwise outstanding quality have been kept for breeding. Mating such a double merle to a black will produce a litter of all blue merles—the only way to do this. One double merle, Merri Lon The Blue Tail Fly, ROM, sired ten champions. Two others, Shadow Hill's Double Trouble and Shamont Ghost of a Chance, have sired at least five champions each. The top blue merle sire in Sheltie history, Ch. Banchory Deep Purple, ROM, was the son of a double merle bitch, Horizon White Ice, bred to a tri-color male. The important thing to realize is that this kind of breeding should be attempted only by a breeder who is knowledgeable about genetics, knows the lines being used well enough to pick outstanding puppies at an early age and recognizes that double merle puppies should *never* be sold as pets unless and until they have been certified by a veterinary ophthalmologist as having normal vision and have been tested and found to have normal hearing. Deaf dogs can adjust quite well

Adding to the interest of color inheritance in the Shetland Sheepdog is the strong presence of blue merle among the allowable colors for the breed. The Sheltie is one of a handful of breeds in which blue merle appears. It is important for breeders to understand the genetic makeup and impact of this attractive color to fully use and enjoy it. That judges like blues is proven by the many good blue merles who have built successful show careers. Such a one is Ch. Shadow Hill's Jazz on Prin Hill, shown taking a BIS at Onondaga under Mrs. Marie Koonts. Tom Coen handled him for owners Larry and Patricia Brunner. *Cirincione*

to a kennel situation, but in a pet home it can be impossible to get their attention.

At one time, Shelties without any white markings were common. Today, however, almost all have white at least on the chest and paws. The genes controlling white spotting in dogs are generally considered to make up a series of four grades of spotting: solid color; Irish spotting, which gives the "classical" collie markings; piebald spotting, which produces fairly extensive colored spots on a white ground; and extreme white spotting, in which markings vary from a colored head and a few colored body spots on a white ground to almost entirely white. The genes show a general dominance pattern of more color dominant over less, but the dominance is not quite complete. Thus a dog with one gene for solid color and another for extreme white may resemble an Irish spotted dog. In Collies and Shelties the dominant gene for solid color seems to have been lost, and all individuals of both breeds have some white markings. All three spotting genes, however, are present in the Shetland Sheepdog, and many of the most flashily marked dogs carry both Irish spotting and a gene for piebald or extreme white. Such dogs are known as white factored.

Although white factoring cannot always be detected, most breeders suspect its presence in dogs with white up the front of the stifles. If two such dogs are mated, a color-headed white (similar to the white Collie) or a spotted Sheltie may be produced. These dogs cannot compete with normal colors under the current standard, but unlike the double merles they are perfectly normal, healthy Shelties in every way and make fully acceptable pets and obedience dogs. The color has been in the breed since its beginning, and every Sheltie alive has white ancestors. In the United States, probably every Sheltie traces in some way to either Ch. Prince George O'Page's Hill, ROM, or Ch. Timberidge Temptation, ROM, one or the other of which is the tail male ancestor of every champion finished in 1989. Both trace tail female to Astolate Lady Harlequin, a white Sheltie with tri-color spots. Not all breeders were happy with the elimination of the color-headed white as an acceptable color, and some are now pushing for a standard change to re-allow this color. The universal presence of white markings on Shelties, by the way, affects the way the black colors are described. Blacks with tan and white are usually called tri-colors, while blacks with white markings but no tan are referred to as bi-blacks. Blue merles with tan markings should be called blue merle, tan and white in contrast to bi-blues which lack tan, but more often blue merle is used as a catch-all term for both types of merled blacks.

It was mentioned above that the black of the Border Collie and probably the black of the early Collie were due to a dominant gene. This may have been true of some of the pre–World War I Shelties as well. By the time the Sheltie was being reestablished in the United States, however, blacks were being produced primarily from matings in which neither parent was black, something which cannot happen with the Border Collie or most other dog breeds. These black-and-white dogs were generally considered mismarked in the United States, even though their color clearly fell into the category of black with white and/or tan markings. During the 1970s several breeders began actively pushing for acceptance of the color by judges, and since 1976, when Ch. Shawn Dar-SummerSong

Stonewall Take Five, bred by Edward Sanchez.   *Jan*

Ch. Cameo The Good Bi Girl, owned by Marilyn and Gene Marlow.

Bi Night and Ch. Carmylie As If Bi Chance finished, black and white has become a very popular color. The history of bi-blue champions is harder to unravel, as the usual designation of "blue merle" gives no information on whether tan points were present. At the least, the number of bi-blue champions has increased greatly in the last fifteen years.

While Shelties generally follow the rules above, there are some notable exceptions. In particular, there are several cases in which a mating of two tri-color Shelties, or of a tri-color to a blue merle, has produced sable puppies, occasionally an entire litter. Another surprise is that many of the double merles used for breeding produce an occasional tri-color. Whether these happenings represent mutations or some oddity of genetics in the breed is at present uncertain.

The only evidence for blue merles in the Shetland Islands is the article by Rev. Oddy, which includes "blue marl" as a color. Other early writers include sable, black with or without white and/or tan, and white with sable markings, but do not mention blue merle. An article published in *The Ladies' Field* in 1917 includes a quote on color from Miss M. Grey, then Secretary of the Shetland Sheepdog Club of England: "The full collie markings are very attractive when they appear in these miniature specimens: white collar and frill, white legs, white blaze and brush tip being much admired both in black and in sable dogs. The black and white dog is a favourite with northern shepherds; the sable and white has its admirers too. Black body colour, the white collie markings, and splashes of tan on face, eyebrows and legs, give a handsome tricolour. Blue merle is as yet unknown in the breed." Regardless of the situation on the Shetland Islands, this certainly looks as if blue merles were not exported to England if they existed.

Maltese blue (seen today in blue Danes, Chows and Dobermans, among others) did occur in the early Shelties, and the earliest "blue" in the Stud Book, Peat, is known from early descriptions to have been an unmerled blue of this type. It is possible that this is the color to which Rev. Oddy was referring. The first blue *merles* in the Stud Book did not appear until 1928, when Kilravock Blue Cloud, a son of the Collie Montlethen Blue Prince, appeared. (Peat, by the way, was a younger full brother of Eng. Ch. Clifford Pat. Eng. Ch. Clifford Pat had descendants registered after World War I, but none was ever imported to the United States and it is almost certain that he has no living descendants today. Peat, however, carries on today in both countries through three sons—including Eng. Ch. Hurley Burley—and a daughter.)

I have traced the merle ancestry of every blue merle in the Stud Book from the first Sheltie listed through the 1960s, and every blue merle imported to the United States until World War II, and found only three sources for the color. The first and most important (almost all U.S. merles, and about half of the U.K. ones) is Montlethen Blue Prince. Although registered as a Sheltie, this dog was identified by Felicity Rogers as "a pedigree Collie with a good show record." The second is Blue Floss of Houghton Hill, a blue merle bitch from a small strain of working Collies from the north of England (originally coming from northern Scotland, possibly of Sheltie origin but very likely crossed with local working dogs). Direct merle lines from both of these Shelties survive to the present in England. The third, Treffynon Tessie, started a merle line that was lost during World War II. Her official pedigree shows her as out of a sable Sheltie by a sable dog suspected of being a Collie cross. The timing of her registration, just as her blue merle daughter needed a pedigree to be exported to and registered in the United States, more than four years after her own alleged birthdate, is suspicious, especially as her breeder was definitely guilty of misregistering other Shelties at about that time. (Eltham Park Anahassitt's official registration shows her as bred by Mr. Pierce [Eltham Park] and whelped just two months after another litter out of her alleged dam. Actually, she was a littermate of Merlyn of Cameliard, and bred by the Allens.) Most likely, Tessie obtained her merle gene from one of the Eltham Park Collies. Another bitch from the same litter from which Tessie was registered, Eltham Park Dinan, was supposedly bred to Eltham Park Blue Sol, a Collie, and the general assumption is that this dog was somehow responsible for Tessie's merle gene.

Ch. Macdega Granada, an attractive blue merle, is owned by the Japanese fancier Kiyoko Mukouda.

Ch. Ashford Promises, Promises, CD, owned by Raymond and Dorothy Christiansen, was Best Veteran Bitch as the ASSA Specialty in 1985 at age twelve.

19

Eye Color in the Shetland Sheepdog

A MAJORITY of Shetland Sheepdogs have brown eyes. A few have lighter, yellowish eyes. Others have blue eyes, and these are variously known as wall, China, watch or pearl. In this chapter we will use the term blue. Some dogs have one brown eye and one blue. An occasional dog will show an iris that is half brown and half blue.

It is the blue eye that puzzles owners and breeders. Much has been written about the inheritance of blue eyes, but almost nothing as to what a blue eye actually is. In this chapter, we will try to explain the nature of color as it occurs in Shetland Sheepdogs.

In nature, basic colors are formed in one of three ways. The first is by pigments; the second by light scattering; and the third by interference. We are hardly concerned with the interference in this chapter. Interference colors are those of iridescence. In the dog iridescent colors occur only in the whites of the eyes, some internal structures and perhaps in the luster of the hair.

Pigments, called melanins, are responsible for all the blacks, browns and grays of the animal world, whether in skin, hair, fur or eyes. Here we are considering only the eye. It is the iris that is "colored" and that therefore gives an eye its color.

The colored portion of the iris is made up of a thin membrane. At the back of this membrane is the uvea. It normally contains deposits of black or brown melanin. These melanins act as light absorbing curtains, and in this way protect the eye from harmful rays.

In the eyes of all brown-eyed individuals, whether people or dogs, there is an additional layer or coating of melanin in the outer surface of the iris. It is this outer layer that gives the eye its color. The melanins absorb the other rays of the spectrum, but reflect back those that we see as brown or black.

Now we have said that the melanins in the uvea are "normally" present. When they are not, then the eye is an albino. Albinism is a genetic error that, fortunately, is rare in Shetland Sheepdogs. Since the melanins are missing, light strikes the thin-walled capillaries and reflects back the pinks and reds of the hemoglobin. Albinos, therefore, have pink eyes.

Now, if the melanins that form the light curtain are present, but are absent in the outer portion of the iris, then the eye is blue. Remember, true blue pigments are extremely rare in animals. And in mammalian eyes, they are totally absent.

The blue of the eye is called structural blue, or Tyndall blue. When we look at the sky on a sunny day, it appears to be blue. The reason is that white light is broken up and scattered. Some of the rays of the spectrum are lost in one way or another. But the blue rays are polarized and beamed to us. Thus, our blue sky is really only the result of having white light broken and scattered by colliding with particles in the upper air.

In considering Tyndall or structural blue, we are dealing with colloidal systems. A colloid is a subdivision of matter in which the particles, often protein molecules, are of submicroscopic size. These particles, which usually range in size from one to 100 millicrons, are evenly dispersed in a medium. Scientists speak of a solid-in-medium, liquid-in-liquid or gas-in-solid medium. All three are responsible for Tyndall blue.

White light consists of all the colors of the spectrum, ranging from the short violet and blue rays to the progressively longer ones ending in red. In the blue eye, there are no black or brown melanins in the outer layer of the iris. So the browns or blacks are not reflected back. The colloidal system then operates. Submicroscopic particles scatter the blue rays, but polarize them in a plane which is in the line of the light beam. The light beam returns to the viewer as blue— structural or Tyndall blue. The quality, that is the depth or the paleness of the blue, depends upon the size of the particles that scattered the blue rays. In some cases, the eye may appear almost white. The larger the particles, the paler the blue will be.

It is possible to extract melanin, or color, from any pigmented tissue. But you cannot do this with any structural blue. You can destroy the color by grinding or crushing the tissue because you have destroyed the light-scattering mechanism, the colloidal system. You might inject a liquid into a gas-in-solid colloidal system and thus cause the blue to disappear. But if the liquid is allowed to disappear, as by drying, then the blue color is restored.

There is a widespread belief that the blue eye in a Shetland Sheepdog is a faulty eye, and that the dog may be subject to early blindness as a result. There appears to be no basis to this, despite the claims of some authorities. It has been argued that blue-eyed Nordics—those from northern countries—must squint a lot

Ch. Banchory Crown Blue, bred by Kathleen Nicks.

Japanese Grand Champion Seamist Notice Me was bred by Michael and Mary Cooke.

Ch. Macdega Oh Mi On Key, bred by Diana Carter.

in order to protect their eyes from the hot sun of temperate or tropical countries.

This claim seems hardly tenable, especially when made in the case of dogs. No light can be stronger than that of the sun upon snow. Many Arctic dogs have blue eyes. Had these been faulty eyes, it is certain that Eskimo breeders would long ago have eliminated the blue eyes from their dogs.

Other authorities have tried to understand the purpose in nature of structural blue, whether in the eyes, skin or hair. They have found no answer. But they have decided that the light-absorbing curtain of the uvea is sufficient protection for the eye. In the Shetland Sheepdog, the eye has additional protection from bright light. It is not set out prominently and it is adequately protected by eyelashes and brows.

The inheritance of eye color is a complex problem. There are many books on genetics that go into great detail upon the subject. Since they are easily available to the student, we will give only a brief generalization here.

True albinism involves the total dog—hair, eyes, skin and internal tissues. Albinos bred to albinos would produce only albinos—in this case, pink eyes. Since no reputable person would make such a mating, it is unnecessary to consider the subject further.

There are only three colors that are common to the eyes of Shetland Sheepdogs. These are dark brown, light brown (sometimes called yellow) and blue. Dark brown eyes are dominant over light brown. Two pure brown-eyed dominants can produce only brown-eyed puppies. But one or both brown-eyed dogs may carry a recessive gene for light brown. In that case, about 75 percent of the puppies will be brown-eyed, and 25 percent will have light brown eyes. If only one of the parents carries the recessive gene for light brown, all the puppies will have dark brown eyes, but about 25 percent would carry the recessive light brown factor.

The problem with blue eyes is more complex and less understood. As we have pointed out earlier, a dog might have two blue eyes, or one brown and one blue. Occasionally, a dog will be seen that has one blue eye and one that is about half blue and half brown. In such cases, the brown is usually dark brown.

Some researchers have felt that blue eyes are linked with coat color, and usually to blue merle. Perhaps a majority of Shetland Sheepdog fanciers have believed this, for the breed standard calls the blue eye a ''merle eye'' and permits them only in blue merle dogs. Others have postulated the belief that blue eyes are in some way linked to tri-color coats. In such cases, they have claimed to see a lighter tan in the hair about the eyes.

Most researchers have noted that blue eyes can occur independently of merle coat color. When blue eyes occur in blue merles many researchers have felt that they are then dominant. But when one or both eyes are blue, and are not joined by a blue merle coat, then the gene for blue eyes must reverse its dominance.

To put it another way, a different set of ''determiners'' must be present to cause a reversal of the dominance. If one eye is brown and one blue, then some

Japanese Champion Backbone of Katsushika Sanyo was bred in Japan by Mariko Yamada.

Japanese Ch. Aliston Purple Choice, owned by Kiyoko Mukouda.

other modifier must be present. And, when the eye is half blue and part brown, either a different set of determiners or a subdeterminer applies.

Whatever the facts may be, the breeding of blue merle to blue merle, and especially when the eyes are blue, is extremely dangerous. Some excellent puppies may result. But many of the pups will be a defective white. Many will suffer from an hereditary disease known as microphthalmia; that is, they may be born with no eyes, or with abnormally small eyes with oblique pupils. Many will be blind, or will shortly become blind. And some may be deaf as well.

20

Shetland Sheepdog Eye Disease

MODERN DOGS are afflicted with a variety of hereditary problems. Among these are eye problems causing blindness. Some breeds, such as Cocker Spaniels, have had a greater than average incidence of glaucoma. Miniature Schnauzers often suffer from hereditary cataracts. Irish Setters, Poodles, Collies, Norwegian Elkhounds and some other breeds have had a terrible scourge known as progressive retinal atrophy or PRA.

PRA ultimately causes blindness. It is difficult to determine in young puppies, so dogs may be used for breeding before the disease is discovered. The disease may appear in any breed at any time. That is to say, it cannot be stated that it will not suddenly develop in some breed that has hitherto had no cases of it.

Although Shetland Sheepdogs seem to be free of this disease, it is necessary to describe it in order to separate it from a somewhat similar problem that does occur in Shelties. PRA affects the entire retina. As the dog ages, the retina begins to lose cells, and to become thinner. There will also be a lack of adequate blood supply, itself caused by the loss of cells. Eventually, the dog becomes blind. The disease is called progressive, because it develops slowly and cannot be stopped. It is called atrophy since the retina is actually wasting away.

PRA is caused by a recessive gene. That is, the gene for a normal retina is dominant. A puppy gets a gene from each of its parents. The pair of genes is called an allele. If the puppy has two dominant genes, DD, then it will have a normal retina. And if two DD dogs are mated, all the puppies will have normal retinas.

If, however, one parent has DD and the other Dd, with the "d" representing the gene for PRA, all the puppies will be normal. But half the puppies will carry the recessive gene for PRA. If two such dogs, both with normal vision, but carrying the recessive gene (Dd × Dd), are mated, then one puppy will be DD normal, two will be normal but carriers (Dd, Dd) and one will have PRA (dd).

If two dogs carrying the dd genes are mated before it is recognized that they have PRA, then all the puppies will have PRA and will ultimately become blind, as will have their parents before them.

There is a similar disease in Shetland Sheepdogs that is a serious problem. It is called Central Progressive Retinal Atrophy, or CPRA. In this disease, the central, or best seeing, part of the retina is gradually destroyed.

A Sheltie with advanced CPRA will be neither night- nor day-blind. It will be able to distinguish stable objects very poorly, or not at all. However, it will be able to see moving objects. This is because the rods and cones in the periphery of the retina have not been affected. Thus, the moving object crosses the retina from peripheral sight, to central retina blindness, to peripheral sight.

Some researchers believe that CPRA is transmitted by recessive genes, as is the case with PRA. But others feel that the reverse may be the case, at least in some breeds. More research is being conducted on this at the present time.

A comparatively recent veterinary discipline is that of the ophthalmologist, or veterinary eye specialist. Such specialists are still comparatively rare, and may not always be within the reach of breeders. Usually, your local veterinarian can tell you where they are located. Or the veterinarian can give you the address of the American or Canadian Veterinary Medical Association, organizations that can supply the information.

Ophthalmologists use an instrument known as the ophthalmoscope. It has a high degree of accuracy in diagnosing both progressive retinal atrophy and central progressive retinal atrophy. The difficulty is that, with the exception of Irish Setters, PRA may be impossible to diagnose until the dog is two to seven years old, depending upon the breed. And CPRA in Shetland Sheepdogs may not be detectable until the dog is two years old. Thus, unsuspecting owners may breed carriers before they are aware of the trouble.

Any Sheltie owner who has any reason to suspect his or her dog has the disease, or is a carrier, should delay using the animal for breeding until a competent specialist can check the eyes, and until the parents of possible carriers have been certified clear.

Recently, a method of diagnosing PRA has been developed, called electroretinography, or ERG. The electroretinogram that is produced will give an absolutely correct diagnosis of PRA in puppies four to ten weeks of age, depending upon the breed. Unfortunately, at the time of writing this method had not been worked out for the diagnosis of CPRA.

There are two excellent sources for information on this. One is the Seeing

Eye Foundation Laboratory of the Cornell Research Laboratory for Diseases of Dogs, Cornell University, Ithaca, New York. The other is the School of Veterinary Medicine, University of Pennsylvania, Philadelphia, Pennsylvania. Research at Cornell was done by Dr. Stephen Bistner and Dr. Gustavo Aguirre. Dr. Aguirre is now at Pennsylvania.

In a personal letter to the writer, Dr. Aguirre makes these points:

> The most successful means of decreasing the incidence of CPRA in Shetland Sheepdogs would be by ophthalmoscopic examination of large numbers of dogs in order to eliminate from a breeding program affected animals.
>
> One of the existing problems in the control of CPRA in Shetland Sheepdogs is in determining the exact mode of inheritance of this disorder. Some individuals believe it to be a dominant trait, but enough dogs have not been examined to determine if there is complete or partial penetrance of the genetic trait. This would be necessary before any measures are attempted to eradicate the disease.

New evidence has developed, and Dr. Aguirre now believes there is evidence that CPRA may represent a dietary factor. It might be possible that a dog might inherit a susceptibility toward the disease, though not the disease itself.

The noted artist L. D. (Ginger) Saksenhaus with Ch. Saxon's Rembrandt, whose show record includes over one hundred BBs and eighteen Group firsts.

21

Character of the Shetland Sheepdog

In CREATING the standard for the Shetland Sheepdog, breeders placed a great deal of emphasis upon temperament. Leaving out the preamble, it is the fourth heading in the standard, and comes after General Description, Size and Coat. This would indicate the importance that early breeders placed upon character, even though only ten points were allowed for it in the Scale of Points at the end of the standard.

The temperament section says: "The Shetland Sheepdog is intensely loyal, affectionate, and responsive to its owner. However, he may be reserved toward strangers, but not to the point of showing fear or cringing in the ring. Faults—Shyness, timidity, or nervousness. Stubbornness, snappiness, or ill temper."

Now the phrase "intensely loyal" is a cliché, a hackneyed and virtually meaningless phrase. At least this is so when it is used to define character in a dog. Every breed fancier in the world claims this quality for his or her breed. Yet how do you define loyalty in a dog? And how "intense loyalty"?

Is a loyal dog one that follows the children to school? Is it one that shadows its master? Will it attack the charging bull that threatens its owner? If the owner engages in a fight with another, will the dog attack the owner's opponent? Will the loyal dog rush into the street and drag a child out of the path of a car?

Dogs do these things. But they rarely have the chance to prove themselves. The dog that shadows its master may do so out of an innate fear of being alone, rather than out of loyalty. Similarly, the dog that barks when strangers approach may be doing so out of fear, and may feel no real sense of loyalty.

Australian Champion Hillacre Hylites in Blue, owned by Hillacre Kennels in Victoria.

Ch. Mountmoor Blue Boy, owned by Mrs. C. A. Ferguson and Miss E. Ford, was Great Britain's top-winning Sheltie in 1988 and 1989.

Similarly, it is a rare dog in any breed that does not show affection for its master and family. This is a quality of being a dog. So, as in the case of loyalty, this really tells us nothing about Shetland Sheepdog character. It is the third word in that description—responsive—that has real meaning.

The major quality in the character of a sheepdog is responsiveness. It must respond quickly to training. It must respond quickly, quietly and without question to commands. And, when herding, it must respond with lightning speed to every move of a wild sheep.

To do this, it must have great powers of concentration. A truism in training dogs, or children, is that you can't teach them unless you can capture their attention. So a sheepdog must give absolute attention to its master during training, and while working in the field. If its attention strays, the lesson is lost or the sheep bolts from the flock and may cause a stampede.

A sheepdog must have a high degree of intelligence. It gains understanding of sheep through experience. But, unless it has great intelligence, it will be discarded by the herdsman long before it has a chance to gain much experience.

Courage can be measured in a variety of ways. A dog that may show fear under certain conditions will show courage under others. The sheepdog must demonstrate its courage in certain very important ways.

It must not be afraid to go far afield in search of a lost lamb. It must show courage when an enraged ram or the angry mother of a lamb charges it. It must not fear to plunge into the flood-swollen waters of a stream. It must not fear to attack wandering dogs that menace the flock.

The good sheepdog has an innate aptitude or instinct for herding. This has been bred into herding dogs since humans first began to change from hunters to agriculturists and herders. Their ancestors for possibly ten thousand years have been herders. Of course, bidability or responsiveness, attention giving and intelligence are all a part of the innate herding aptitudes. Still others are nipping at the heels, rather than biting or slashing, and silent fighting. The noisy fighter might cause the herd to stampede.

Shetland Sheepdogs have been impressive in obedience trials. Many of them win highest scoring dog in trial honors. They show the result of those thousands of years of breeding for such qualities as response.

Obedience training and trial do not, in the author's judgment, demonstrate intelligence, or even require it. But they do demonstrate other character qualities—attention-giving, trainability, response, steadiness and obedience to command.

"However," says the section on temperament, "he may be reserved toward strangers." This is again a quality that belongs innately to a sheepdog. Such dogs live on lonely farms. They have work to do, and they know it. They may have to work in gales of rain or snow, and they must work to a large extent alone. So it is natural that they should be reserved, or suspicious, of strangers. Moreover, the demand for good herding dogs has always been great. One not suspicious of strangers would be easily stolen, and it could as easily be sold on a "no questions asked" basis for a high price.

Ch. Lencrest Renegade o'Tara Hill, owned by Dorothy Aldrich. *Graham*

Ch. Raetta's Mark of Jobe, owned by Henrietta Huston. *Petrulis*

Ch. Catamount Black Phantom, owned and bred by Mr. and Mrs. Stanley Saltzman. *Tauskey*

These are some of the positive qualities in the character of the Shetland Sheepdog. It is true that few, if any, ever get a chance to demonstrate them in sheepherding trials or in actual farm work. But the author cannot believe that a thousand generations of breeding for innate aptitudes can be eliminated in a few show generations. But they can be nullified by serious character faults.

Over the past two decades, there has been a remarkable change in Shetland Sheepdog disposition. The shyness and cringing that were so common in dogs entering the ring have disappeared, replaced by alert, friendly dogs that demonstrate ideal Sheltie character. This has been true even with six-month-old puppies that have been trained by experienced owners or handlers.

However, novice owners are apt to bring inexperienced and untrained dogs into the show ring. This chapter should prove useful for the novice, but it also provides information on Sheltie character and temperament useful to any Sheltie owner.

Judges are often amused by the imagination used by exhibitors to excuse shyness. But after a time, they get simply bored. They've heard all the phony reasons. Here are some of them.

"He is not used to men." "He won't show in a building." "He's not used to showing on grass." "The last judge squeezed his testicles." "Another dog lunged at him just before we entered the ring." "He doesn't like to have you open his mouth." "He fell on the ice and skinned his testicles, so he won't let you check his rear end." "This is his first show." "He's only a puppy." "He's got a phobia on women's skirts." "Ever since the vet gave him a shot, he's been afraid of people in white." And so on, ad infinitum.

As a judge, it has not been the writer's experience that Shelties are fear biters. Some may cringe away in fear, but they do not try to bite. This is quite different than the situation in some other breeds in which there are dogs that will try to bite the judge.

Snappiness is, perhaps, a different type of character fault. Thus, the Sheltie on our farm will try to bite you if you try to clean its ears or trim its toenails. And many veterinarians report that Shelties try to bite them when they are being treated.

This is not necessarily a fault in Sheltie character. It can be poor training on the owner's part. It is natural for dogs to use their teeth. Millions of dogs have to be taught that they are not allowed to bite human beings. And they *can* be taught this. But hundreds of thousands of doting owners fail to discipline their dogs.

It is a part of sheepdog character to be possessive. The dogs had to be possessive of the sheep they herded. They had to know the limits of the farm or grazing lands. They had to keep the sheep from straying onto another's property, and to keep strange animals and people off their land.

Such dogs may be possessive of the food dish, of their beds, of toys. But they can be taught that they must not be; that the baby can take away the toy or food dish, or crawl into the dog's bed.

We did not know the Sheltie on our farm when it was young. Nor does it

Ch. Starhaven's Rainbow Brite, shown with handler Carl Langhorst, is owned by Joseph Molloy and Amy Langhorst. *Bergman*

Ch. Genre Here Comes the Son, owned by Carol Groff, is shown here with handler Meredith Maust. *Meneley*

live in our house now. So we had no chance to train it. But we did have the Belgian Sheepdog from its puppyhood. Belgians are somewhat sharper by nature than are Shelties. Or, perhaps we should say that Sheltie character is of a gentler sort.

We had to teach the Belgian that she had to permit us to cut her nails, and that she could not bite if hurt while combing out hair mats. When she would be hurt, she would yelp and turn her head to bite. Turning the head is the first step toward biting. So we disciplined her sharply. Then we tried to show her that we did not mean to hurt her, and that we would be as gentle as possible. Now few dogs are so gentle.

This is the sort of training that any dog can receive. Were it given to all Shetland Sheepdogs, the vast majority of them could not be faulted for snappiness or ill temper.

There are two other characteristics that should be discussed. One is nervousness, and the other is stubbornness. The first is almost always a hereditary fault. Highly nervous dogs, and those that are actually hysterical, should not be used for breeding. The standard requires that they be faulted in the show ring. But breeders should make no excuse for them, and should guarantee that they do not spread their faults further in the breed.

Many breeders make the excuse that ''she'll be all right after she has a litter.'' She won't be. And neither will her puppies be. As a rule, the puppies will be more shy than their dam is.

Whether stubbornness is a fault is a debatable point. Stubborn dogs are often hard to train. But once trained, the stubborn dog may be a gem. It will not quit when herding during gales. It will work until exhausted. And while it may be lacking to some degree in intelligence, it will make up for it by following orders perfectly.

However, if the stubborn dog dislikes dog shows, its stubbornness may prevent it from winning. It will refuse to cooperate with its owner and handler. In that sense, stubbornness is certainly a fault.

If one enters a home that has Shetland Sheepdogs, the dogs will normally dance just out of reach of the newcomer. This is not generally a form of shyness. It is a form of caution that has been bred into sheepdogs for thousands of years. They dance just out of reach of strangers who might steal them. They also dance just out of reach of the rams and wild sheep that might butt or charge them.

Recently, a Sheltie breeder put it this way: ''People have got to learn that Shetland Sheepdogs are not Cocker Spaniels. It is not in their nature to fawn upon strangers. Nor should it be.'' In determining the character of their breeding stock, Sheltie owners should make this distinction between true shyness, true fear and the prudence that Shetland Sheepdogs should possess.

Shelties often remain vigorous into advanced age. The dog shown here is Ch. Merriley's Steely Dan, and in this photo he was an incredible twelve years old. An American, Canadian, Mexican and international champion, he also held the coveted OTCH designation. Of Dan's 136 BB wins, thirty-six came after his twelfth birthday. This spectacular senior citizen was owned by Karen and Gene Dickinson and is shown with his handler, Pam Shea. *Missy*

22

About Measuring Shetland Sheepdogs

SIZE IS A PROBLEM in Shetland Sheepdogs today as it always has been in the past. The standard calls for the disqualification of all dogs that are under or over the desired heights, that is, under thirteen or over sixteen inches at the highest point of the shoulders. This disqualification applies only to dogs in the show ring.

When registering dogs the American Kennel Club ignores height, as it does also brindle color (brindle is also a disqualification). If a Sheltie is a brindle ten inches tall, or a brindle twenty inches tall, the American Kennel Club will register it so long as its papers are in order.

The American Kennel Club does, however, set up rigid rules for dogs that enter the show ring. At the present writing, any exhibitor competing in the ring at the time can demand that a competing dog be measured. Or, the judge can himself measure the dog.

At one time AKC rules required that a measuring committee be set up in advance by the show-giving club, and this committee would measure the dog. The owner was not allowed to participate. Dogs were measured by a sort of guillotine affair that was set over the dog at the highest point of the withers. Then a bar was lowered and set on the shoulders under the hair. The bar was then locked in place. Only one measurement was permitted.

Few dogs could tolerate this. They cringed, or actively fought to escape. The measurements were thus not accurate. But they were used for that show. If the dog was measured at the next two shows, there would be three different measurements.

Am., Can. Ch. Rosewood Collector's Item, HC, owned, bred and shown by Rosemary Petter. *Lindemaier*

Am., Can. Ch. Jerbo's April Sunrise, owned by Mr. and Mrs. Jerry Owens. *Lindemaier*

I then devised my own system. I obtained ⅟₁₆-inch rods at a hardware store and bent them to three sides of a square so that they looked like croquet wickets. Then the ends were cut off to produce one thirteen-inch and one sixteen-inch wicket. I took these to the show, and if I thought a dog was over or under size I used the wickets.

At first the AKC howled, saying that this violated the rule against more than one measurement and, in any case, only a duly formed committee could do it. The answer was that the dog was not actually being measured, but only a determination was being made to see if it should be measured.

Eventually, the AKC came around. It had the present adjustable wickets made. And it changed the rules so that the judge would do the measuring. If the dog is within the standard, the judge marks his book "measured in." If it is too tall or too short, the judge marks his book "measured out, disqualified." The dog is then dismissed. This is good for that show only. If the dog is disqualified at three shows, then it cannot be shown again.

The AKC wickets are extremely expensive, far too expensive for even major breeders. But breeders can make their own wickets, such as I have described, for a few dollars. There is then no excuse for showing a dog that is over or under the standard heights of thirteen and sixteen inches.

Now there are some moral considerations involved. The height disqualifications were made by the American Shetland Sheepdog Association after a long and bitter battle with the American Kennel Club. It is therefore the duty of responsible Sheltie breeders and exhibitors to see that the disqualifications are enforced.

The trouble is that many exhibitors think that it is poor sportsmanship to demand that another dog be measured. Some, while being sure that a competing dog is over or under, will not demand a measurement until the last second, when it seems certain that the dog is going to win. To make the demand at that stage is indeed "dirty pool."

But the judge also has a responsibility to measure questionable dogs. He is a custodian of the standard, and he should live up to his responsibility. The trouble is that some judges are afraid to measure a dog for any reason. They feel that it will bring the ill will of exhibitors. But experience has shown that most exhibitors will praise the judge. And since there is now no excuse for showing an under- or oversize dog, the exhibitor who shows a dog of nonstandard height will reap the anger of the other exhibitors.

There is one other point that should be made. Requests for the measurement of a dog in the ring must be made by an exhibitor or handler while in the ring.

Ch. Marwal Steppin' Out, owned by Diane Bostwick, has a number of outstanding wins to his credit. The presentation of one of the most coveted awards is shown here—Herding Group first at the 1990 Westminster KC show. The judge was Dr. Quentin La Ham, and presenting the Strathglass Trophy for the Club is Mr. William Chisholm. The happy handler is Cheryl Willacker. *Ashbey*

23

How to Groom Your Shetland Sheepdog

by Barbara Curry

IN DISCUSSING GROOMING with a number of Shetland Sheepdog breeders who show their own dogs, and with two professional handlers, all said that Mrs. Barbara Curry of Beltane Kennels had written the finest article ever produced on the subject. We therefore asked Mrs. Curry to write this chapter.

Mrs. Curry says modestly that she has learned much from Collie fanciers as well as from Sheltie exhibitors. While her article deals mainly with preparation of the Sheltie for the show ring, it is equally valuable for those who do not exhibit, but who want always to be proud of their dogs.

Mrs. Curry's article is substantially the same as one she wrote some years ago for the *Sheltie Special.*

GROOMING THE SHELTIE FOR THE SHOW RING

Just as many paths may lead to the same road, so may different methods of grooming result in the same finished product. The grooming methods described herein have been developed after much trial and error by the author, who feels that you do your dog an injustice when you take him into the ring poorly groomed.

ALL trimming should be done at home a day or two before the show, leaving only coat preparation—which takes no more than thirty to forty-five minutes, depending upon the amount of coat carried by the dog—to be done at the show. It is not necessary to do the trimming one to two weeks before the show to allow for growth of hair to cover the mistakes. Trimming techniques should be practiced and perfected by the novice on a dog other than one being currently exhibited. All trimming should be done in such a subtle manner as to appear to be the normal growth of hair. When one trims the skull, for example, to the point where it becomes obvious, one might just as well hang a sign on the dog pointing out to the judge the fault one is supposedly trying to minimize.

The tools needed for trimming are a thinning shears (with double thinning blades), barber's scissors, stripping knife and a fine-tooth comb, along with the normal steel comb set with medium and coarse teeth.

Trim the feet first, removing the hair with the barber's scissors from the area between the large heel pad and the toes. Grind down the toenails with either a grinding appliance or steel file. With the scissors trim the hair around the foot even with the nails. If there is a large amount of hair growing between the toes, hand-pluck this out with your fingers. Older dogs have a tendency to grow "snowshoes" between the toes. If this is allowed to occur it will spread the feet, and when removed leave a gap between the toes. It is best to keep this removed all the time to prevent the spreading of the toes.

To trim the back pastern, comb the hair with the fine-tooth comb straight out and use the thinning shears to trim it, rounding it out evenly with the heel pad. The use of barber's scissors leaves a "scissored" look, while the thinning shears, which take longer, gives a more natural appearance. Use the thinning shears on the back of the front pastern also, cutting the hair close at the heel pad and tapering it into the longer feathering on the front leg.

Head trimming is difficult and the area where many overdo it. Clean out the long hairs on the inside of the ear with the thinning shears, and drastically reduce the large tuft of hair in front of the ear, taking several cuts with the thinning shears and combing out to see the result before proceeding further. Do not remove the hair that frames the front of the ear, but just clean away the long straggly hairs and the thick tuft mentioned above. The back of the ear should be handplucked, again to remove the straggly hairs. If the ear carries a very heavy coat and tips too far, excess hair may be removed with the stripping knife or the thinning shears. Avoid "doctoring" the back of the ear too much, as it is readily visible. Where the inner corner of the ear joins the skull one usually finds a long growth of hair. Grasp the ear in the one hand and extend the ear away from the head, creating a straight edge, which may then be trimmed with the thinning shears. Low-set ears may be made to appear higher set by trimming some hair away from the outer ear edge. If the ear is properly set, leave this area alone, as the longer hair here helps to frame the face.

Carefully remove the whiskers and mole hairs (over the eyes, on the side of the head and under the jaw).

If the dog is wider in skull than desired, or carries a thick growth of hair on the sides of the skull, trim the skull as follows. Picture a triangle, from the corner of the eye to the lowest point where the ear joins the skull, and from the

Ch. Four Clover's Black Orphee, CD, owned in Japan by Yoshio Mori.

Am., Can. Ch. September The Provider, owned by Masayuki Noguchi.

Can. Ch. Carmylie Dance to the Music, owned and bred by Jean Simmonds.

Ch. September Easy Street (Ch. Barwood Cabriole Razor's Edge ex September Magic Maggie McGee), owned and bred by Barbara and Kenneth Linden.

When a successful show dog is also a successful producer, it is truly a happy combination. Here Ch. Marwal Steppin' Out (second from left) joins three winning offspring from one litter for a family portrait. They are (from left) Teaberry Lane Makin' Whoopee; Steppin' Out; Ch. Willow Layne Makin' Out and Am., Can. Ch. Willow Layne Makin' Time.

Ch. Macdega The Chrome Pony, owned in Japan by Kiyoko Mukouda, was bred by Debra Tessman and Thomas Coen.

Ch. Barwood Cabriole Sky On Fire, owned by Marjorie Norstrom, was Hawaii's top Shetland Sheepdog winner for four years.

corner of the eye to the highest point where the ear joins the skull, the base of the triangle being the ear itself. This is the area to be thinned out. If one examines the dog, one will see that (except in the tri-color) the hair is light at the base and darker at the end. The darker color forms the mask in the sables. If the hair is cut at the base, it will not be missed. If just the black portion is removed, the light part will show, leaving a gap in the mask. This is where the trimming becomes obvious. Therefore, the hair must be cut at the base, and this can be done only with the thinning shears. With your hand, make a part in the hair and lay the thinning shears against the skin, taking only one or two cuts. Comb out before going further. Repeat this procedure, making new parts, and staying within the triangle. This will trim out the side of the skull above the level of the eye, without it becoming noticeable.

The side of the head below the level of the eye can also be trimmed out by inserting the trimming shears into the mass of thick heavy hair and laying it as closely to the skin as possible, combing out and surveying the results frequently. Proper skull trimming on the short, wide-headed dog will give the illusion of a longer, leaner skull.

After all trimming is done, brush the dog thoroughly, *to the skin*, using a bristle brush. Pin brushes are fine to remove dead coat on the shedding dog, but are not recommended for the healthy coat, as it does do some damage. Brushing out to the skin, separating each and every hair, takes longer with a bristle brush, but does not damage healthy coat. Train the dog to lie quietly on his side while you meticulously part the coat and brush it out. Then turn him over to do the other side. This procedure is essential on heavy-coated dogs if the dog is to appear in the ring "without a hair out of place." If the undercoat is clumped, the dog will look "lumpy."

After the dog has been thoroughly brushed out, put him in the tub and wash the white areas only, with tepid water and shampoo. Occasionally one sees the dog whose coat still appears lumpy in spite of thorough brushing. This is usually caused by an accumulation of oils from the skin and the only solution is a complete bath. There are risks with bathing, however, for if the dog is due to shed, the bath will hasten shedding. It is perfectly safe to bathe a dog just coming into a new coat.

At the show, first prepare the white areas with Foo-Foo Powder (available at the concessions) and precipitated calcium carbonate (available at the drugstore), mixed half and half. After spraying the legs lightly with water and rubbing to distribute the moisture evenly, apply large amounts of this mixture with a teasing brush, working it in against the lay of the hair (place an old towel on the grooming table to collect the excess, removing it after the whites are done). If the dog does not have white legs, apply plain Foo-Foo sparingly, working it in with the fingers or brush. Leave all the excess powder temporarily on the legs and proceed to the collar and skirting. Spray the collar lightly and distribute the moisture evenly with your hands. Sprinkle heavily with baby powder, working it into the coat with your free hand as you sprinkle. (Foo-Foo can cut coat and should therefore not be used liberally on the collar. Although

144

Am., Can. Ch. Cataway's Swiss Aire, CD, HC, owned by Cataway Kennels, is shown in a BB win at the Harrisburg KC under judge Muriel Sonnichsen, handler Patty Page.　*Ashbey*

Ch. Minos Fame N' Fortune, CDX, owned by Karen (handling) and Gene Dickinson and Chris Gabrielides. A BIS winner in three countries, he is shown taking the top prize at the Silver Bay KC of San Diego under judge John Honig. James Frank presents the trophy.　*Bergman*

Ch. Lobo Dell's Charm Bracelet.   *Ludwig*

Ch. Rorralore Mickey Dazzler, owned by Charlotte Clem McGowan.

Am., Can. Ch. Roydon's Queen Kandi, owned by Roydon Shelties.

baby powder may soften the coat, it does not damage the coat when used as frequently as is necessary when campaigning a dog.) Then rub it in thoroughly with both hands. Spray the skirting in the back and the underside of the tail and repeat the same process with the baby powder. Now remove all the excess powder. Use the teasing brush and brush the legs against the lay of the hair until all the excess powder is removed and the legs are dry. Comb out the back pastern with the fine-tooth comb. To remove the excess powder on the collar, face the dog and start at the lowest point of the bib, holding the hair above it out of the way with your left hand. Brush down vigorously toward the table, and in this manner work your way up to the chin and around the collar. *Be certain to remove all the excess powder!* This method whitens and brightens the white areas, setting them off from the body color, adds "bone" to the legs and separates and fluffs out the collar.

If the dog has a blaze, chalk it heavily with a piece of white chalk, including the underjaw, and then use a hand towel to wipe off the excess. Put a small amount of petroleum jelly on your finger and apply to the nose, making a straight line across the nose so that the blaze is well-defined from the nose. Put a small amount of petroleum jelly on the fingers and rub your hands together and then smooth down the sides and top of the skull. (If you apply too much it can easily be removed with the towel.)

Spray the body coat with water. If the coat has been thoroughly brushed the night before the show, it is not necessary to dampen the coat heavily, which requires longer drying time and more brushing. A moderate amount of water, distributed throughout the coat with the hands, will provide enough moisture to "stand" the coat up. Brush the dog vigorously with the bristle brush toward the head, including the belly coat and thighs, also brushing up the collar, until it is fairly well dry and all the hair well separated. Use the rattail end of the teasing brush to work the show lead in out of sight directly behind the ears. Take the dog off the grooming table and encourage him to shake and settle the coat in place, and then place the coat over the hips in proper place with the wide-tooth section of the steel comb.

Am., Can. Ch. Happy Glen's Royal Dream, CDX, HC, owned and handled by Barbara Ross, has BIS wins in the U.S. and Canada. Here he is being presented with BIS at the Bonneville Basin KC by the author. This good win was scored from the classes. *Missy*

24

How to Show Your Shetland Sheepdog

THERE IS a rather special art to showing a Shetland Sheepdog. Since the writer of this book is an all-breed judge, what is said below is based partly on how the good professionals and amateurs show their Shelties, and partly on how judges want them to be shown. Since, as a rule, the judge first sees the dogs in action—in gaiting—let us discuss this first.

Judges customarily send the dogs in each class around the ring once or twice before having them posed (''set up'' or ''stacked'' are terms often used). Judges may then have the dogs gaited before having them posed, or they may have them posed, examine each dog individually and then may gait them. Some judges may take each dog separately from the group, examine it and then gait it.

Gaiting usually consists of having the dog trot away from the judge, and then back. The judge will stand in such a position that the dog is moving back and forth directly in the judge's line of vision. Some judges, particularly in classes of one or two dogs only, may require a triangle pattern. That is, the dog moves away along one side of the ring. It then crosses the far end of the ring, then comes back to judge diagonally.

Still others want a T pattern. In indoor shows this is most often used when the center mat forms rectangles on each side of it. The dog is then sent out on this center mat. It is then taken across the far end mat, back across again, and then is returned along the center mat. This method will give the judge evidence of the dog's ability to cover a lot of distance with the fewest number of steps.

It is the exhibitor's job to study the judge's ring methods, note the procedure used, and then follow it. You can do this by watching part of the judging of a previous breed, or the earlier judging in your own breed. A judge must make hundreds of decisions during a day's judging, and must shrug off many annoyances and irritations. One such annoyance comes when an exhibitor, say the fifth in the class to be gaited, asks: "How do you want me to move?" If the judge wishes to see your dog gait in any pattern other than those used by the preceding dogs, he will tell you.

In gaiting, the judge is trying to determine correct angulation and movement of the forequarters. The elbows should be tight to the body. The legs slant inward slightly so that the pad of one foot might almost but not quite touch the print of the other. When the dog is moved at a fast trot, the legs move inward toward the centerline of the body. This is called single tracking. There should be no crossing over of the feet during either the slow or the fast trot.

Some dogs single track, and especially if pulling on the leash. In such cases, the front legs appear to move in to a single forward line which would represent the center balance line of the dog's body. There would be no true crossing over. Usually a dog on a tight lead—"strung up," as the saying goes—both single tracks and crosses over. And, moreover, the dog cannot be kept along a true course. At a fast trot a Sheltie will single track naturally.

The hind feet, too, may tend to single track at a fast trot. There should be no crossing over. The hock joints should not be so close together that the feet drive outward instead of straight forward. When the feet drive outward, the dog is using energy to move its feet away from the line of forward motion. It is also losing ground with each step.

Crabbing, or side-winding, is also a serious fault of gait. The dog does not move forward in a straight line. The rear end is swung slightly to the right or left, so that the body is actually diagonal to the true line of forward motion.

Crabbing may be the fault of the handler. It may be due to a fault of conformation. Or it may result from lack of experience. When not due to conformation, crabbing can be corrected. The dog needs plenty of experience at gaiting so that it doesn't unconsciously pull itself out of line. Since most indoor shows use mats, the dogs are required to move along on them. This suggests a way of training your dog.

Try gaiting your dog along the edge of a sidewalk so that, if it doesn't move in a straight line, its rear end will fall off the edge of the walk. Or work with it along the street, and very close to the curb. If you work along the curb, then keep your dog close enough so that it is almost crowded against it. If on the tree lawn, then close enough so that its rear end will fall over if it does not go straight. Your goal is double: to get the dog to move in a straight line beside you, and to do so on a loose leash.

Judges and breeders often complain that many Shetland Sheepdogs have a stilted gait; that is, they move forward with mincing, prancing, almost dancing steps. The Sheltie is a working dog. It should reach out with its forelegs and then drive hard with the hind legs. Part of the trouble can be yours. You move too

Ch. Lassen Best of Times, owned and bred by Ann and Sam Neftin and co-bred by Carolyn Stone, was BB at the 1989 Santiago Shetland Sheepdog Club Specialty in an entry of 263 under breeder-judge Barbara Linden, handler Lisa Laguire. *Bergman*

Ch. Show Biz Kleeland Star Struck was BB at the Milwaukee Specialty under judge Donald Henderson, handler Lloyd H. Graser, Jr. *Booth*

151

Am., Can. Ch. Sandalwood's Beach Bunny, HC, owned and handled by Linda Churchill, was BB in 1987 at the Del Valle Dog Club from the classes under breeder-judge Charlotte Clem McGowan. *Fox & Cook*

Am., Can. Ch. Gallantry Solid Success, owned, bred and handled by Mona Stolcz, was Best of Winners at the Evergreen Specialty under judge Harrison Fagan en route to his American title. *Lindemaier*

152

slowly, and the dog keeps pace with you. Speed up a bit. Teach your dog to move forward as fast as it can without breaking into a gallop.

Most Shelties are posed in such a way that they stand truly, look upward at the exhibitors and carry their ears at alert. Since Sheltie ear placement, size and correct tilt of the tips is so important, you can't expect to win unless you can "alert" your dog. This is done by "baiting." Usually the exhibitor keeps the dog's attention by teasing it with a bit of boiled liver, or even a bit of dog biscuit.

The exhibitor teaches the dog to stand while on a loose leash. The handler stands in front of the dog and holds the bait in one hand. If the dog tries to move forward, the handler moves a knee forward so that the dog must stop. The dog is thus kept in relatively good position, as far as head, ears, neck and front legs are concerned.

But if the dog is continuously moving forward, the exhibitor is in danger of backing into the dog ahead of it. In such cases, many inexperienced exhibitors tend to turn toward the edge of the ring, thus presenting the rear of the dog to the judge. But, whether the handler turns toward the outside of the ring or toward its center, the judge is given a three-quarters view of the dog when a full profile view is wanted.

If your dog does get out of line, tighten your leash, take the dog out of line, make a reasonably large circle, and then replace the dog as it should be. The judge may wish to see all the dogs posed for a front view. If so, be alert for this, and turn your dog so that it faces the judge.

If the class is large, the dog may become impatient. In such cases, give it a nibble on the liver or biscuit. Give it just enough to get it interested again. Be sure that the hand holding the liver is directly in front of the dog, so that its head is not turned to either side.

Many Sheltie exhibitors concentrate too intensely upon getting the front legs set truly and the ears alert that they forget the rear end entirely. Consequently, they may not be aware that the dog has moved one or both rear legs forward and under the body. The hocks are too far under, the rump is too high, and the dog appears to have a sway back.

In training, glance back occasionally at the hind end. Train yourself to be aware of the instant the dog moves a leg out of position. When this happens, tighten the leash, hold it in such a way that the dog will keep its head up, and then reset the hind leg. This is done by grasping the leg at the stifle joint, lifting it slightly and placing it in position. This requires considerable training since the first few times you try it, the dog will move—and probably because you pulled it out of position.

Many an exhibitor complains that the dog stands and moves perfectly at home. But then they add such excuses as: "He doesn't like the leash." "He doesn't like to show inside." "He can't stand to have strangers go over him." "He won't let anyone look at his mouth." "He can't bear to have anyone touch his testicles."

In most cases, these are really excuses for lack of training. When you are training your dog, make sure that it is hungry—at first, very hungry. Then when

Ch. Badgerton Alert Alec, a BIS winner during the late 1950s, owned by Tobruk Kennels. *Tepe*

Ch. Lingard Catamount Cameo, owned by Mr. and Mrs. Stanley Saltzman.

Ch. Shanteroo Black Jack.
Mikron

Special events at dog shows add to the fun and teach spectators a little extra about the breeds they see. The Tacoma KC offers a costume show and the second-prize winner in 1989 was Barbara Kuhl as a Highland fiddler accompanied by her Ch. Strathspey Eavesdropper and Ch. Miapooper of Mistyglen's, CD. *Ross*

Karen Hostetter furnishes a vital service to the fancy with the Shetland Sheepdog Library. Here she joins some of her own dogs for a family portrait.

Wherever brace classes are offered, Shelties are likely to appear. The breed matches up well and the dogs work well together. Here Sandmere Diamonds in the Sky (left) and his son Sandmere The Skylark pose for the camera with owner-handler Louella Ericksen after a Group victory.

Ashbey

Four Shelties can work as well as two. Here Best Team in Show at the Long Beach KC show consisted of (from left) Tabur's Ricky Racer; Tabur's Ima Elegant Lady; Dan Dee Sunwest Honey Vanilla, CD, PC; Mex., Int. Ch. Sunwest Thru the Lookingglass, CDX, PCE, HC, HT, STD, owned by Dr. Lynette E. Rath. The judge was Charles Rupert and Charles Long presented the trophy for the club.

Ludwig

the training lesson is over, it is fed. If you do this regularly, the dog will begin to look forward to training because it knows that it will get fed, or at least get delicious snacks, as soon as the training period is over.

Always take the dog to the show hungry. Give it snacks when it leaves the ring, plus plenty of petting and praise. It is not unusual to see people hug and pet their dogs even when the dog has done no better than to get fourth in the class. Tomorrow, the dog might win. And alertness in the ring may be a major factor.

Thus far, we have said nothing about the examination the dog must undergo. The dog must not pull away from the judge. Neither should it cringe. The judge will want to see the teeth. It is a courtesy to him if you pull up the lips, or open the mouth for the judge. Apart from the courtesy, you may be preventing the spread of disease.

The judge must check for soundness of front, eye size and color, ear size and placement, shoulder placement, back roached or swayed, angulation at the stifle, the testicles, hocks, coat texture, etc. If the dog cringes, the judge will have difficulty and you may lose. Yet you can condition your dog to stand this examination and even to enjoy it.

As in other training, the dog should be hungry, and should be rewarded afterward. Each member of the family should go over the dog as you have seen dog show judges do. And this should be done repeatedly. Always *afterward*, the bit of boiled liver or the biscuit snack should be given. Finally, strangers should be asked to use your procedure. At first, have them do it in your own home, then on the street.

Your dog must also become accustomed to strange noises, strange buildings and strange dogs. So take your dog to shopping centers. Praise it when people pet it. Remember to do this when it is hungry, and to feed it upon return home. Take it for long walks. Accustom it to car riding. And take it to sanction match shows where it can meet and get used to being around many dogs.

When you take your dog to its first show, take it when the show opens, even if you are not judged until afternoon. This will give it a chance to settle down, to get used to the building, the loudspeakers and the strange dogs. After you've been judged, stay until the end of the show.

Am., Can. Ch. Markrisdo's B.A.'s Patt'chez, owned by Charles and Patti Bruce, was a well-known herding champion during the late 1960s. He is shown here in a conformation win under judge Rutledge Gilliland.

Roberts

25

Working Trials on Sheep

There is no good flock without a good shepherd
And no good shepherd without a good dog.

THE QUOTATION above is taken from the French Shepherds Club, and it is also the motto of the Shetland Sheepdog Trials Association of the Shetland Islands, Scotland. So far as the writer has been able to determine, this is the only club in the world that gives sheepdog trials exclusively for Shetland Sheepdogs. And one would be less than truthful if he did not admit, that, today, Border Collies do more sheepherding in Shetland than do Shetland Sheepdogs. Even in the islands, one constantly hears such things as: "Shetland Sheepdogs are only toy dogs," or "They are only show dogs."

J. A. Reid, a successful breeder and competitor in sheepdog trials for working, or Border Collies, wrote the article on working Collies for Brian Vesey-Fitzgerald's *The Book of the Dog*. He dismissed the Shetland Sheepdog in these words: "Nor need anything be said about the so-called 'Shetland Sheepdog'; for it is not a worker but merely, in the main, a miniature show Collie, and as such, is a production of yesterday." Thus does he dismiss both the Collie and the Sheltie.

And yet, just after World War I, Shetland sheepmen were determined to save the great little workers that had for so long herded their sheep. Thus, in 1923, the Shetland Sheepdog Trials Association was formed. It has held trials every year since. These trials do not differ in any respect from those given for Border Collies. And the dogs that compete are the equal of the Border Collies.

Perhaps here, we need to give some qualifications to the above remark. No dog is better than its trainer, just as no trainer can be a winner without a dog that lives up to its trainer. The ability of any dog to win is based on the perfection of its unison with its trainer. More trainers work with Border Collies, and so it may be possible that more of them are better trainers than are their opposite numbers among the Sheltie owners. It is also true that the Shetland Islanders are not professional trainers. They are herdsmen who compete with their private working dogs, as much to determine future breeding stock as to win prizes.

The original Shetland working dogs were much larger than those of today. They were called Haad Dogs. They were used to chase, trip, throw and hold wild Shetland sheep until their masters could tie them. But such dogs and such methods disappeared with the advent of Scottish shepherds (the Shetland Islands were once Norse). The Scottish shepherds brought their own dogs, and they had already developed modern means of controlling sheep with dogs.

Again, to be truthful, we must admit that the Shetlanders speak of two breeds of Shetland Sheepdogs, even though both might be registered under the one breed name. There are the working Shelties and the show Shelties. The former are selected for self-reliance, intelligence, trainability and stamina. Herdsmen boast that the dogs can run sixty miles in a day and do the work of twenty men. Show Shelties, they say, are selected chiefly for show points, and only afterward for temperament. One can draw a parallel between the modern field dogs, such as field-bred and bench-bred English Springer Spaniels. They are so different in appearance and in working abilities as to appear to be different breeds. There is, however, less difference between the working and the show Shelties.

Competition is keen. The 1972 trials were held at Swinster, Tingwall. There was a junior class for "boys and girls under 18." The Limit Class was for dogs that had not won a prize in the open class. The Open Class was open to "all dogs not entered in the Limit Class or eligible for the Championship Class; also the first three prize winners of the Limit Class." The Championship Class is confined to the prize winners in last year's class, and the first three prize winners of the Open Class on the day of the trials. There is also a Doubles Class.

In all, fifty dogs competed. They performed before a highly knowing, or expert, audience and before an outside judge. The winner of the Champions Class was C. R. Nicholson of Weisdale with a dog listed only as Glen. Glen took second in the Open Class to Roy, a dog brought over from Aberdeen on the Scottish Mainland by his owner, Andrew Sutherland.

Before indicating the tests given to working sheepdogs in trials, the author would like to insert a personal comment. He judged as many as ten thousand dogs a year of all breeds. He attended, and sometimes judged, a variety of sporting dog field trials. And he has attended sheepdog trials on three continents. He does not think the Shetland Sheepdog can be sold so short. Shelties are trainable and biddable, and most of them have a high degree of intelligence. So it cannot be taken for granted that they would fail if given a chance, from weaning, at sheep work. Their background as workers is still too intense for that.

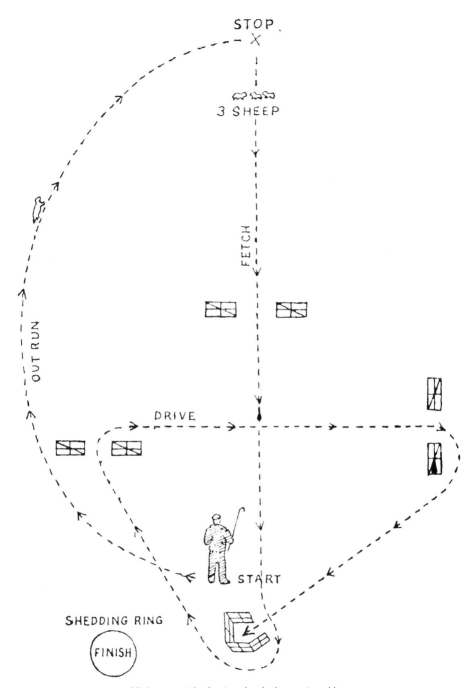

STOP
X

3 SHEEP

FETCH

OUT RUN

DRIVE

START

SHEDDING RING

FINISH

All dogs must be kept on lead when not working.

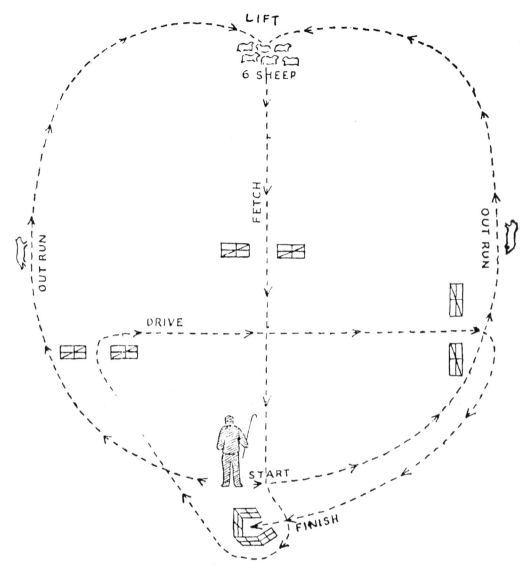

Each dog is expected to keep its own side and do its fair share of the work.

Still, Sheltie breeders and exhibitors, and especially those interested in obedience, should attend sheepdog trials. They would find the performances simply breathtaking. And they would gain a new concept of obedience work. Dogs may be sent off by an imperceptible (to people) movement of the foot, or by an almost inaudible hiss. They may drop instantly on a hand signal, or to a whistle. They anticipate the moves of wild sheep, and when they think the sheep are alarmed, they may drop and remain absolutely still until the sheep have calmed.

Sometimes at winter shows, such as Westminster, Border Collies demonstrate the penning of wild sheep. But the writer has seen Kelpies herd three-day-old chicks into tin cans; has watched Border Collies send sheep down a chute at a speed which just allows a man to force the sheep's mouth open and shove a worm capsule down its throat before the next sheep comes along. The dogs will herd geese. And they will not hesitate to run over the backs of closely milling sheep when it becomes necessary to get them moving in the right direction.

The trials given on Shetland do not differ greatly from those given for Border Collies in the British Isles, the United States, Canada, Australia and New Zealand. A dog will have to go out on the "outrun," that is, take a circular run until it gets in back of some wild sheep some two hundred yards straightaway from the shepherd. It must then drive the sheep—three at Shetland trials—directly toward the shepherd, between two gates, around a pen behind the shepherd, then through another gate. It must then drive the sheep at right angles, across to the other side of the course, through a gate and then into the "shedding ring" behind the shepherd.

In brace stakes, two dogs go out on the "outrun" on opposite sides of the course. They must get behind the sheep, which are at a greater distance from the shepherd than in singles trials. All six sheep must then be herded over a course similar to the one described above, and must then be penned.

At international championship trials, dogs might have to go out as far as eight hundred yards, and each dog of a brace might have to pen ten or twenty sheep. Other tests are correspondingly difficult.

Have Shetland Sheepdogs ever been used for herding sheep in the United States? Have they ever competed in sheepdog trials in this country? The answer to both questions is "yes." However, they have been used sparingly. They had to compete against already established breeds—the Border Collie and the Australian Shepherd (a breed now unknown in Australia). Their records in sheep herding are mostly unknown, for such records were never kept.

Louise Knowles of Brookridge Kennels, Gunnison, Colorado, was an early Sheltie breeder and her family owned a ranch. In 1943 Miss Knowles bought Pixie Pan of Laurelridge from Mr. and Mrs. Ben Cooley of Laurelridge Kennels, Hillsboro, Oregon. The dog lacked one point for its championship. The Cooleys had just imported Ch. Laird of Exford. Miss Knowles had Pixie Pan bred to Laird before she was shipped to Colorado. She whelped seven puppies, four bitches and three males.

Three of the pups were kept for use on the Knowles Ranch. "They didn't need any training to be good stock dogs,'' she writes. But let her tell of the litter.

One was sold to a sheepman here in Gunnison. He always took his sheep to high range for the summer, and this was the first time he had had a dog to help with the sheep. He had a herder who stayed with the sheep. About every two weeks, the sheepman would take food and supplies to the herder. And he also took food for the dog.

One of the times the sheepman took food to his herder, he became very ill. The herder had to stay with the sheepman until he could get word to someone to get an ambulance up there to bring the man to the hospital. It took six days before anyone passed by so that the herder could get word to the doctor. The little dog, Wee Cadet of Brookridge, took the sheep from the bed ground every morning and brought them back at night without losing a single one from the flock.

After he had got his sheep down from the range, the sheepman sold both his sheep and the ranch. Since he didn't want to keep the dog in town with nothing to do, I bought him back. Many of the ranch men wanted him, but they wouldn't pay my price. They all said that no dog was worth that price.

Another pup went to a family here in Gunnison to be a pet for a two-year-old youngster. She made a wonderful pet for the child. She wouldn't let the child catch her and wool her. She just kept far enough way from the little boy to keep him from reaching her. There were several little children in the neighborhood and they all played together. They would run around the block, and the puppy herded them as she would have sheep or cattle when they are being driven to a certain location.

She was named Pixie after her mother, and people called her Little Pixie. Little Pixie wouldn't let any of the children get off the sidewalk. The mothers knew that when Pixie was with the children, they were well taken care of.

I sold Wee Foxy to a farm family in Kansas. She always went with the man when he went out to the barn to do the chores. One morning, one of the cows ran after the man and knocked him down and began trampling him. If Foxy hadn't been with him, the cow would have killed or seriously injured him. But Foxy diverted the cow's attention and got her away so that the farmer could escape.

I sold a pup from another litter (Pixie had been bred again to Ch. Laird of Exford) to a dog trainer in La Junta, Colorado. He trained all breeds of dogs. This dog was named Trinket. And when this trainer got Trinket, he wrote me that she was the easiest dog to train he had ever trained.

He trained Trinket for sheep trials and entered her in one in Utah. She had to compete against all breeds of sheepdogs. The dogs had to work rams. And as more dogs worked them, the rams became meaner and more difficult to handle. Trinket worked late in the trials. She was the only dog which was able to corral all the rams. But to do this, she had to get a bit rough with them, and the judge refused to give her the winner's points. She was never entered again.

The trainer to whom Miss Knowles refers is Don Evett. He operated a dog training school for some years. He confirms what Miss Knowles has said about Trinket.

''I never had a dog easier to train,'' he says. ''In fact, she really trained me. I used her for years to train the other dogs. She was one of the few that was not timid, and she was wonderful to handle.''

Sheepdog trials were first held in Great Britain just one hundred years ago. They began in the United States some two years later. One of the clubs organized at that time was the American Sheep Trial Club. It was organized in Oregon and it has held trials ever since.

Though it is not as well known as other clubs, trials have been held on member club ranches from time to time. Dogs competing have been Border Collies, Australian Shepherds and a breed known locally as the Black and Tan Shepherd.

Shetland Sheepdogs were considered to be only "Toy Collies" and, as one man expressed it, "more toy than anything else." It was not until 1966 that a Shetland Sheepdog proved the contrary. The dog who did this was Markrisdo's B. A.'s Patt'Chez, generally called "Patches."

He was sired by Am. & Can. Ch. Malpsh the Duke of Erle out of Am. Ch. Markrisdo's Highlands Wendy, and he was bred by Mr. and Mrs. C. A. Buckmiller of Markrisdo Kennels, Beaverton, Oregon. Charles and Patty Bruce of Kelso, Washington, bought him, and Mr. Bruce trained and handled him.

During the next four years, Patches won the herding championship of the club, defeating Border Collies, Australian Shepherds, the Black and Tan Shepherds and other Shetland Sheepdogs that were attracted to the trials. In all, he won all the thirty-three trials in which he competed. A perfect score is 200, and Patches never scored lower than 195.

He won three trials in 1970 before being injured while successfully shoving a child out of the path of a car. The dog was something more than just a herding dog, however. The Bruces owner-handled him to both his American and Canadian bench championships. He was ten times Best of Breed, and got one second and one fourth in group.

Butine's Summertime Taffy, UD, Can. CDX, owned, trained and handled by eleven-year-old Sandy Merinsky, taking the high jump with style and enthusiasm. The youngest person ever admitted to membership in the Bayshore Companion Dog Club, Sandy was also invited to compete in the Gaines Superdog Classic.

26

Shetland Sheepdogs in Obedience

OBEDIENCE TRIALS were designed to counteract the wide-spread belief that ''show dogs are beautiful but dumb'' (meaning stupid). Almost immediately, the trials turned out to be a fascinating and fun-filled additional activity for the owners of purebred dogs. And they have done much to convince the general public that the owners of purebred dogs are responsible citizens who do not let their dogs become public nuisances.

We have already remarked that Shetland Sheepdogs have three great qualities—a high degree of intelligence, an aptitude for training and what we can call ''bidability''—the willingness to obey. No dog can be trained in obedience until it will give absolute attention to its owner or trainer. Nor can it win unless it will obey instantly and correctly. Most Shelties fit these qualifications.

Obedience work should be taught to every Shetland Sheepdog whether or not it is to be entered in a show, or in obedience competition. The well-trained dog is always a great joy to its owners, and a cause for neighborhood pride. Most cities and towns have primary obedience training classes. In these, the dogs learn to obey such simple commands as to come when called, to walk at heel on or off the leash and to sit and lie down upon command.

Some of these dogs go on to advanced training. Many enter competition at the shows. But those that do not are still a source of pleasure and pride to their owners. They help to improve the image of both dogs and dog owners in their home neighborhoods. And, of course, they advance the Shetland Sheepdog as a breed.

It is not our intention to give an exhaustive report on obedience procedures. There are excellent books available on this, including the training of the dogs. But a short outline is in order. Obedience work is divided into four divisions: Novice, Open, Utility and Tracking. Dogs getting three qualifying scores in the novice classes win a Companion Dog (CD) title. They may then compete in the open classes. When the dog gets three qualifying scores in these classes, it earns a Companion Dog Excellent (CDX) title. It can then compete in the utility class. Three qualifying scores are required to win the Utility Dog (UD) title. Tracking tests are given in open country. If the dog passes, it can add Tracking Dog (T) to its titles.

In recent years, the AKC has created a new title, or degree, that of Obedience Trials Champion (OTCH), and it has made competition possible in two exciting and fun new exercises, brace and team events. There is also a veteran's class.

Only dogs with UD degrees can compete for an Obedience Trials Championship. Consult the AKC booklet, *Obedience Regulations*, amended on March 1, 1989, for full details. Note that as of April 1990, 1,600 plus dogs had won UD or higher titles

Before obedience trials were formally adopted by the American Kennel Club, the American Amateur Training Club was organized at Chicago. It then permitted the organization of a Cleveland chapter. These clubs were basically for Doberman Pinschers and German Shepherds. When the American Kennel Club formally established obedience trials, the Cleveland chapter became the amateur training division of the Western Reserve Kennel Club. Thereafter dogs of all breeds were permitted to enter for training. The sole qualification was that the dog should be purebred. However, puppies had to be six months old, or older.

It is not surprising then that the first Shetland Sheepdog to win a UD title was a Cleveland area dog. Her name was Beach Cliff's Lizette. She was bred at the Merrilynn Kennels of Basil and Agnes Benson. The Bensons had been Collie breeders before adding Shelties. Basil Benson had been a long-distance (twenty miles) Lake Erie swimming champion, and as was Ella B. Moffit of Rowcliffe Kennels, he was also interested in Spaniel field trials.

Lizette was whelped April 25, 1936. She was by Ch. Pegasus O'Pages Hill out of Longleigh Merrilynn. The Bensons sold her to Mrs. Irma Werner of Beach Cliff Kennels at six weeks of age. At eight weeks old, Lizette would, upon command, dive into a fish pool.

Mrs. Werner had been a German Shepherd fancier since her childhood in Denmark. She became an early member of the Cleveland training group. When World War II came, she became a member of the Dogs For Defense Cleveland chapter. And she was one of those who gave basic training to the dogs that were then to be sent to Army war dog training units. Counting German Shepherds and Shelties, there was a time when more than a dozen of her champions had one or more of the obedience titles.

Ripple Laddie became the second Shetland Sheepdog to win a Utility Dog title. He was bred by Margaret Perry of Hancock, New Hampshire. He was

Ch. Starhaven's Rockin' Robin, CD, owned by Carl Langhorst.   *Kelly*

Dreamalot Stephi Mignonette, CD, HIT winner, shown with Karen Hostetter.

whelped April 7, 1938, by Sheltieland Little Tartan out of Flagstone Tess. Eleanor S. Lundberg trained him and campaigned him to the UD title. Both Lizette and Laddie competed in the days before the tracking test was added by the American Kennel Club. In the lists given below, they are considered to have won this also, since they had won all they could.

It is hard to realize now the sensation these two dogs created. They were competing in a branch of the sport that, except for a few Poodles, was considered to be the domain of the German Shepherds and Doberman Pinschers. These two dogs did much, therefore, to open the classes to all breeds. And, of course, they did much to promote the Shetland Sheepdog.

Many Shetland Sheepdogs have won highest scoring dog in show honors. So it is hard to single out one dog as having been the greatest of all. We do, however, single out one dog as a perfect example of what the Sheltie can do. She is Ch. Wee Lassie of Eve-Bart, UD, owned by Mr. and Mrs. Dan Kerns of Center Valley, Pennsylvania. Note that she is a champion and a UD title holder. She was the nation's top obedience dog of all breeds in 1970. Moreover, she is the first champion in any breed to earn the title of top obedience dog, all breeds, in the United States. She is by Lonnie Du of Eve-Bart out of Wendy of Eve-Bart.

Through 1972, 387 Shetland Sheepdogs have won Utility Dog titles. Many others have won one or more of the lower titles, and some have passed their tracking test as well. Obviously, the number of dogs winning the UD title is much less than the number winning the CDX, which, in turn, is fewer than those winning only the CD title. At least one thousand have won the CD title.

Sheltie Champions and Utility Dog Titlists to 1973

1. Ch. Geronimo Little Gremlin
2. Ch. Sea Isle Wee Bairn
3. Ch. Badgerton Flirt
4. Ch. Prince Patches of Feracres
5. Ch. Pameron's Copper Penny
6. Ch. Astolate Emblem of Merit
7. Ch. Merrywood's Candy of Pintura
8. Ch. Geronimo Little June
9. Ch. Sheldor Honor Guard
10. Ch. Blue Beau of Pocono II
11. Ch. Kawartha's New Gal in Town
12. Ch. Mr. Sunshine of Teradane
13. Ch. Playmate's Beau of Teradane
14. Ch. Sea Crag's Golden Bonnie
15. Ch. Lingard Danwyn's Gay Miss
16. Ch. Shalimar's Donnybrook Fair
17. Ch. Wee Lassie of Eve-Bart
18. Ch. Dreamalot Max
19. Ch. Marjan's Teddy of Scarlet Oak
20. Ch. Nodsoc Taro Blue Thunder

Sheltie Champions and Utility Dog Titlists 1973–1989*

Ch. Al-Dors Partial Eclipse, UD (1981)
Ch. Amstad Aleta of Glyn-Ayre, UD (1985)
Ch. Ashley Grove's Chief Justice, UD (1988)
Ch. Banchory Silver Thaw, UD (1979)

* Dogs are alphabetical. Year after name is year of either the Champion or Utility title, whichever was published last.

Ch. Sea Isle Rhapsody of Halstor, owned by Edith Overly.

Thornedge Mainstay, Am., Can. UD, owned by Dorothy Remen.

Ch. Beltane Joshua's Trumpet, UD (1989)
Ch. Benayr Bonfire, UD (1976)
Ch. Blue Springs Sweet Sage, UD (1978)
Ch. Camelot's Morgan LeFay, UD (1983)
Ch. Cee Bar Spark of Succession, UD (1989)
Ch. Christy of Honeywood, UD (1982)
Ch. Cypress Blue Buccaneer, UD (1978)
Ch. Donlyn's Silver Lining, UD (1988)
Ch. Flair Ace-In-The-Hole, UD (1978)
Ch. Flair On Parade, UD (1979)
Ch. Glen-Nel Hallmark O'Noradel, UD (1987)
Ch. Harvest Hill's Tom Jones, UD (1986)
Ch. Heather Glen As Handsome Does, UDT (1973)
Ch. Highfield's Edge of Dawn, UD (1980)
Ch. Highfield's Summer Thunder, UD (1985)
Ch. Hylati Prince Hottentot, UD (1984)
Ch. Jakeland's Court Jester, UD (1985)
Ch. Jo-Lyn's Special Edition, UD (1982)
Ch. Lanbur Good Times Murph, UDT (1989)
Ch. Lobo Dell Tangerine Fizz, UD (1981)
Ch. Lobo Dell's Charm Bracelet, UD (1975)
Ch. Marjans Teddy of Scarlet Oak, UD (1973)
Ch. Miapooper of Misty Glen's, UD (1985)
Ch. Millbrook MacAlester Lad, UD (1988)
Ch. Mirluc I'm A Handsome Devil, UD (1986)
Ch. Moribrook's Upsy Daisy, UDT (1981)
Ch. Nodsoc Cimarron, UD (1981)
Ch. Prelude's The Intruder, UD (1988)
Ch. Prelude's the Perfectionist, UD (1989)
Ch. Schoodic Helzablazen, UD (1975)
Ch. Scotchguard Challenge, UD (1975)
Ch. Sea Isle Clancey of Sagebrush, UD (1978)
Ch. Sheltara's Classic Fashion, UD (1985)
Ch. Sheltara's Solid Gold, UD (1985)
Ch. Simmore Genuine Sat'Sfaction, UD (1988)
Ch. Stonerhaven's Flaunt It Flolyn, UD (1988)
Ch. Sundene Sable Sensation, UD (1989)
Ch. Tagalong Normandy Pirate, UD (1984)
Ch. Trelane Woodwyn Enterprize, UD (1989)
Ch. Westernesse Megan O'Lobo Dell, UD (1983)
Ch. Westernesse Orange Blossom, UD (1986)
Ch. Westernesse Windswept, UD (1985)
Ch. Winsawn's First Choice, UD (1988)

Ch. Hi-Hope's Merry MacDuff, Can. UD, and Ch. Hi-Hope's Merry Imp, CDX.
Allen

Ch. Wee Lassie of Eve-Bart, UD, owned by Daniel Kerns, was a leading obedience performer.

Ch./OTCH Scotchguard Champagne (S. Hoelzle) (June 1978 & July 1978)

Ch./OTCH Donlyn's Gypsy Gambler (Whitler & Munsey) (December 1977 & March 1980)

Ch./OTCH Merriley's Steely Dan (K. Dickinson) (September 1976 & June 1982)

Ch./OTCH Benayr Grelore Fleetwood Mac (K. Dickinson) (January 1980 & August 1986)

American Shetland Sheepdogs with UDT Titles to 1973

*1. Beach Cliff's Lizette
*2. Ripple Laddie
3. Sea Isle Little Tinker
4. Christopher Boy
5. Sandy of Brunhal
6. Ch. Sea Isle Wee Bairn
7. Pameron's Little Rascal
8. Sheltie Glen Shagbark
9. Minden
10. Golden Cove Shadow
11. Torlea's Brinda
12. Gail Patricia O'Pages Hill
13. Dusty Chiquita
14. Chiquita's Suzanne
15. Astolat Mr. Wonderful
16. Phillida of Hillswick
17. Hooligan of Orchid Lake
18. Tenorap's Lady Luck
19. Gillian O'Hillswick
20. Ch. Sea Crag's Golden Bonnie
21. Grayfield Peach Brandy
22. Carla's Little Peek-A-Boo

Obedience Trial Champions†

OTCH Abbie Lee Fancy
OTCH Ace of Spades
OTCH Adelheid To Linderhof
OTCH Amstad Regimental Piper
OTCH Andromeda's Bi Black Brandy
OTCH Andromeda's Doze' Em Over, TD
OTCH Ardyth Absolute Corker
OTCH Astolat Rob Roy of Hillndale, TD
OTCH Astolat's Myrrdin Embrys
OTCH Aurora-D's Special Angel
OTCH Aynsworth's Gimminy Cricket
OTCH Bach's Flirtatious Lady
OTCH Bar-Dow's Sassy O'Sheltara
OTCH Barker's Amber Enchantress
OTCH Bertic's Royal Randy

OTCH Bevan's Rustic Scottsman
OTCH Bo-Ed Nifty of Windrem
OTCH Bonnie Charles Krug of Flair
OTCH Bonnie Heather-Lyn
OTCH Bonnie Tarabrandy
OTCH Brujean's Trace of Beauty
OTCH Calcurt Twinkling Starlight
OTCH Caleb's Skyler King
OTCH Caledon Short Notice
OTCH Car-A-Lam's Eze Rider
OTCH Car-A-Lam's Snapdragon
OTCH Catamount Rainy Day Blues
OTCH Catamount Socks V Meadowrock
OTCH Cathy's Molly
OTCH Cee Dee's Starr, TD
OTCH Chantey's Jewel of Mirluc

---

* Dogs 1 and 2 are included because they won the highest training awards possible in their day, before Tracking degrees were officially awarded.
† The OTCH title was begun in 1978; dogs are listed alphabetically; ILP dogs are not counted.

Can. Ch., OTCH Clan Lasslyn Carry The Day, Am. CDX, expertly clearing the bar jump.

Can. Ch. Beddington's the Tempest, CD, TT, is also a BIS dog. Tempest is owned by Debra Morash and Donna Laye.

OTCH Chenterra Jubilation
OTCH Cherryglen Gal Friday
OTCH Cherryglen Sum Pumpkin
OTCH Cheyenne Indian Love Call
OTCH Cindy's Jenny of Grape St.
OTCH Courtney II
OTCH Dash O'Ginger of Bydand, TDX
OTCH Dentwoods Rhododendron
OTCH Donlyns' Delightful Mindy
OTCH Donlyn's Johnny Be Good
OTCH Dorlane's Jessica
OTCH Dunlaps Kringles Elf
OTCH Elf Dale Apache Blue
OTCH Elf Dale's Pied Piper
OTCH Elf Dale's Spinner of Dreams
OTCH Flolin's Sir Scottie
OTCH Flolyn's Whim Wham Man of Rolin
OTCH Forelyn Puddle Jumper
OTCH H Bar Sass N Brass
OTCH Halterburn's Firestorm
OTCH Heather Glen Nick O'Gold
OTCH Heather Glen's Charlie
OTCH Highfield's First Frost
OTCH Highland's Prince Michael
OTCH Hillswick MacLeod of MacLeod
OTCH Indiancreek Starfall Keeper
OTCH Ivy House Celebration
OTCH Jakeland's Magic Marker
OTCH Jakeland's Sparkling Embers
OTCH Jazzman of Emerald Isle
OTCH Jo-Lyn's Big D
OTCH Jo-Lyn's Bronco Buster, TD
OTCH Jo-Lyn's Chip Off The Old Block
OTCH Jo-Lyn's Chipper-At-A-Boy
OTCH Jo-Lyn's Jubilee O'Greeley Glen
OTCH Jo-Lyn's Nathan
OTCH Jo-Lyn's Painted Poppy, TDX
OTCH Jo-Lyn's Sacee Sensation
OTCH Jo-Lyn's Snap Crackle N Pop
OTCH Jo-Lyn's Texas Tornado

OTCH Jo-Lyn's Tri A Little Magic
OTCH Jo-Lyn's Varsity Ace, TDX
OTCH Jo-Lyn's Whiff
OTCH Jo-Lyn's Winter Snowflake
OTCH Kinion's Star of Shanarra
OTCH Kynos Dapper Dan of Damalee
OTCH Laddie of College Park
OTCH Laddie of San Shel
OTCH Lamar Silver Shimmer
OTCH Leolair's Aldebaran D'Hyades
OTCH Li'l Miss Mary, TDX
OTCH Lobo Dell Elrond of Rivendell
OTCH MarJan's Jocko Joel
OTCH Marriott Tonight
OTCH Me Luv Vincent Van Go Al-Dor
OTCH Mystical Misty of Ryan
OTCH Namesake's Valentino
OTCH Oh Mi Bodacious Thunder
OTCH Patrician Honey's Dear Kelly
OTCH Patti Anne Sachie
OTCH Penelope Lee of Encino
OTCH Peter Pan of Naripa
OTCH Piper's Toby O'Archer
OTCH Playboy's Gold Dust
OTCH Pomeroy's April Delight
OTCH Primrose Merrie Melody
OTCH Raintree's Nre Frontier
OTCH Ramblewood's O'Shea of Shilo
OTCH Rebel Charge, TD
OTCH Roanoke's Tessie
OTCH Rosewood's Baron of Hy-Verta
OTCH Royal Scamper
OTCH Ryshan's Rock and Roll
OTCH Sabrina Nicoles Dawn
OTCH Sage's Kissin Cousin
OTCH Sandi-Lon's Endora
OTCH Sandi-Lon's Kool Hand Luke
OTCH Sandmere Tommie's Legend
OTCH Sandy's Sparkling Spanky
OTCH Seago's Tiny Tip
OTCH Shamont Spirit of Christmas
OTCH Shelley Bonnie Lassie
OTCH Sheltara's Carina Ann
OTCH Sir Ralph De Bricassart

The world's most titled dog is Ch. Simmore Genuine Sat'sfaction, UD, shown here with his owner, Jean Schmidt. In six years this Sheltie has won every title in conformation and obedience open to him in the Bahamas, Bermuda, Canada, Chile, Costa Rica, the Dominican Republic, Guatemala, Mexico, Peru, Puerto Rico and Venezuela. He has won at three World Shows and the great Las Americas shows for a total of fifty titles.

Agility is catching on rapidly in the United States today and Shelties have a natural talent for it. Here a puppy owned by Marianne Higgs works on some of the apparatus, preparing for its future.

Alician Hiland Midnight Piper, Am., Can. UD, UKC UUD, demonstrates the weaving poles exercise in agility work for owner Marianne Higgs.

Canada has also taken warmly to agility. Here a member of an agility team watches as her Sheltie goes through the scent hurdle exercise in an exhibition at the Fort Garry KC, Saskatoon, Saskatchewan.

OTCH Skoof Blue Sky After The Storm
OTCH Sooner's Sacee Sean
OTCH Starhaven's Now or Never
OTCH Starmist Tymtel's Miniken
OTCH Tamaron Tinkerbelle O'Tino
OTCH Tangle Glens Good Time Bess
OTCH Tenorap's Bold MacDuff
OTCH Tevroc Midnight Altar Boy
OTCH Tha-O-Vil's Golden Cricket
OTCH Thelroy's Frederick The Great
OTCH Tiee Hall Wild Shenanigans
OTCH Trace's Travlin Reflection
OTCH Twin Oaks Fantasia
OTCH Windowshadow's Master Yoda, TD
OTCH Winetime Blu It
OTCH Winetime's Fancy Raisin
OTCH Worthington's Misty Shadow

Ch. Rhodan's The Windwalker, owned by Kathleen Schmutz, has many fine wins on his record, including first in the Herding Group at the Westminster show in 1985 under breeder-judge Dona Erich Hausman. He was shown by Guy Mauldin. *Carter*

Ch. Lanbur Garden Party, owned by Mary A. Hayes, is a multiple BIS bitch.

27

The Great Winners

THERE IS A SAYING that records are made to be broken. There is another that says that the greatest dog in the world may be in someone's backyard—unknown to the show-dog world. What the former means is that there will always be someone ready to shoot at, and go over, the current record. The second saying needs some adaptation to the present subject.

A great dog may appear, shine brilliantly, then disappear. Any number of things can happen. The dog may become ill and be retired, or it may suffer an injury. The owner may be unable to show the dog in an appreciable number of shows. The dog disappears and is quickly forgotten. Anyone who has remained in dogs for a period of years will remember several such cases.

But these cases cannot in any way lessen the brilliance of the dogs that do make the records. They appear in show after show. They are always in tip-top condition. They stand travel perfectly. Their temperaments catch the eyes of the judges. They face the best dogs of their time, and they win. In short, they are remarkable.

Given below are the names of the great winners, past and present.*

Ch. Albershel Brigand (D-S), Jenks
Ch. Aynsworth's Kilts 'N Tartans (D-S), Raven & Buchman
Ch. Badgerton Alert Alec (D-S), Dewitt
Ch. Balenbrae Buck Rogers (D-S), Rejholec
Ch. Banchory Back Stop, ROM (D-T), Oishi & Parker

---

* Sex and color of dog are in parentheses.

Ch. Kismet's Centurion, owned by Guy and Thelma Mauldin, shown being awarded BIS at Clearwater, Florida, in 1973 under the author.

(Ch.) Banchory Formal Notice, ROM (D-T), Harden & Moffatt
Ch. Banchory in Dress Blues (D-B), Norris
Ch. Banchory Rebel Blue (D-B), McConnell
Ch. Banchory Thousands Cheered (B-B), Harden & Bosse
Ch. B'fields Bublin' Champagne (D-S), Zwart
Ch. Birch Hollow Once Upon a Time (B-S), Nicoll
Ch. Blue Quest of Pocono (D-B), Reed
Am. & Can. Ch. Bob's Mt. Piper O'Tentagel (D-S), Reeves, Fletcher & Paterson
Ch. Brackley Born to Shien (D-T), Boyette
Ch. Brandwell's Break-A-Way II, ROM (D-S), Page's Hill Kennels
Ch. Brandywines Bounty Hunter (D-S), Braithwaite
Ch. Brangay Unchained Melody (B-S), Tacker
Ch. Cahaba's Som 'N Special (D-S), Waldo
Ch. Cameo Fantasy In Blue (B-B), Robinette
Ch. Chenterra Farmer Boy (D-S), Kortkamp
Ch. Chenterra Thunderation, ROM (D-T), Barger
Ch. Chisterling Ricochet (D-S), Combee
Ch. Chisterling Scarlett O'Hara (B-S), Laverty
Ch. Conendale Challenger O'Akirene (D-T), Hubbard
Ch. Dan-Dee's Mandy of Clelland (D-S), Holcomb
Ch. Dark Miss O'Page's Hill (B-T), Levine
Ch. Dawn Heir's Striking Starlet (B-S), Sherrill & Youmans
Ch. Elf Dale Viking, ROM (D-S), Sanders
Ch. Esquire's The Claimjumper (D-S), MacNamara
Ch. Esterline's Rain Dancer (D-S), Stahl
Ch. Flair Phoenix Blue, CD (D-B), Valo & Cabbage
Ch. Grelore Believe It (D-S), Grahm & Virden
Ch. Grelore Village Goldsmith (D-S), Reese
Ch. Halstors Peter Pumpkin, ROM (D-S), Coen
Ch. Happy Glen's Royal Dream, CDX (D-S), Ross
Ch. Hatfield's Stardust (B-S), Clem-McGowan
Ch. Hi Road Trifecta (D-T), Glang
Ch. Honeybun's Blackjack (D-T), Meger
Ch. Kankun's Li'l Swinger (B-B), Harris
Ch. Karelane Royal Flush O'Kismet, ROM (D-B), Samuels
Ch. Karral Good Times, ROM (D-S), Elledge
Ch. Kensil's Saddle Tramp (D-S), Gillis
Ch. Kismet's Centurion (D-S), Mauldin
Ch. Kismet's Saint or Sinner (D-S), Mauldin
Ch. Knightwood Wynborne Breeze (B-S), Knight-Marshall
Ch. Lanbur Garden Party (B-S), Hayes
Am. & Can. Ch. Laurolyn Patti O'M-B (B-B), Mori-Brook Kennels
Ch. Legacy Steels Breese (D-B), Howard
Ch. Lobo Dell Bear-Cat (D-S), Girton

Ch. Sutter's Golden Masquerade, owned by Dona Erich Hausman.

Am., Can. Ch. Cee Dee's Squire, CD, owned by Mr. and Mrs. Don Henderson.

Ch. Wyndcliff Richmore Striking, owned by Joan Surber.

Ch. Meadows Fire of Bryce Star-Lit, owned by Pat Meadows. *Bergman*

Can. Ch. Banchory Birth Right, CD, owned by Mona and Lisa Stolcz.

Ch. Stonerhaven Primrose Lane, CD, owned by Philip and Judith Parrillo, has won a host of BBs and Group placings. *Meneley*

Ch. Rockwood Repeat Performance, owned and bred by Barbara Kenealy. *Krook*

Am., Can. Ch. Banchory The Candidate is a son of Ch. Halstor's Peter Pumpkin, the top sire in the breed in the U.S. and Canada.

Ch. Luv's Special Touch (D-S), Waldo
Ch. MacDega Canden Coming Home (D-S), Coen
Ch. MacDega Sultana (B-B), Coen
Ch. MacDega The Family Man (D-S), Coen
Ch. Mac's Sir Thomas (D-S), McKintyre
Ch. Malpsh Great Scott, ROM (D-S), Hays & VanWagenen
Ch. Marwel Steppin' Out, ROM (D-S), Bostwick
Ch. Mau-Land Stormy Weather (D-S), Sabourin
Ch. Meadows Fire of Bryce Star-Lit (D-S), Meadows
Ch. Merriley's Steely Dan (D-B), Morley & Dickinson
Ch. Merrywood Lance O'Shadow Hill (D-S), Merrywood Kennels
Ch. Minos Fame 'N Fortune, CDX (D-S), Dickinson & Gabrieledes
Ch. Mistimoor Stonehenge (D-S), Flessas
Am. & Can. Ch. Mori-Brook's Country Squire (D-B), Mori-Brook
  Kennels
Ch. Mori-Brook's Icecapade, CD (D-B), Martin
Ch. Mus-Art's Vive Vega Vive, CD (D-B), Adkins
Ch. Noralee Leader O'Roc-Sycamore (D-S), Martin
Am. & Can. Olympic Fairy Flower, CD/ROM (B-S), Miller
Ch. Phildove Kismet Heir Borne, ROM (D-B), Brody & Mauldin
Ch. Pixie Dell Epicure (D-S), Barker
Ch. Pixie Dell Little Gamin (D-S), A. & M. Miller
Ch. Prairie High Plains Drifter (D-S), Geister & Wolcott
Ch. Ray Eden's Ricardo (D-S), Ray
Ch. Rhodan's The Windwalker (D-S), Nakahara
Ch. Robrovin Johnny Appleseed (D-S), Still
Ch. Rockwoods Gold Strike (D-S), Kenealy
Ch. Roc-Sycamore Minute Man (D-S), Martin
Ch. Romayne's Autumn Fireside (B-S), Danforth & Sevigny
Ch. Romayne Special Edition (D-S), Kramer
Ch. Rorralore-Sportin' Chance, CD/ROM (D-S), Wadsworth & McGowan
Ch. Rosewood's Christy the Clown (B-B), Petter
Ch. Rustic's Delightful Penelope (B-S), Worsham & Segelike
Ch. Sea Haven The Sorcerer (D-S), Samuelson
Ch. Shadow Hill's Jazz on Prinhill (D-B), Hammett
Ch. Shal-Dan Shel-Lee's Blue Lagoon (B-B), Humphrey
Ch. Shamont Ruby Slippers (B-S), Coen
Ch. Shelando Rion Bright Sunrise (B-S), Rice & Bromley
Ch. Sir Joshua of Winslow, ROM (D-S), Chandless
Ch. Skyways Sa-Wen (D-B), Walters & Mauldin
Ch. Sue Rich's Bandit of Sarwyn (D-S), Sargeant & Adams
Ch. SummerSong Winter Shadows, ROM (D-B), Haderlie
Ch. Summerwynn Charm O'Roydon (B-S), Yamashite
Ch. Sundials Pegasus (D-S), Carothers
Ch. Sundial Rendezvous (D-S), Carothers

Am., Can. Ch. Mori-Brook's Icecapade, CD, owned by Mrs. Lee O. Martin and bred by Mori-Brook Kennels. This renowned blue merle is shown in a Group win under judge Derek G. Rayne (center).

Ch. Chisterling Ricochet, owned, bred and handled by veteran fancier Donald Combee, was Group first at Asheville, 1988, under judge Eleanor Evers.

Graham

Am., Can. Ch. Mori-Brook's Country Squire, owned by Mori-Brook Kennels, had a long, illustrious career. He is shown here scoring a Specialty BB under judge Miss E. M. Babin at the amazing age of fourteen and a half years. *Booth*

Ch. Sunnybrook's Matchmaker (D-S), Cram

Ch. Sunnydell The Dream Weaver (D-S), Anderson & Gabrieledes

Am. & Can. Ch. Sutter's Golden Masquerade (D-S), Daniels & Hausman

Ch. Tantera Dayspring Crescendo, CD (D-S), Zupann & Maust

Ch. Tiree Hall Jedelan Scot (D-S), Hendrickson & Newland

Ch. Tull E Ho Miss Fire (B-S), Tull

Ch. Tull E Ho's Valentino (D-S), Jaquez

Ch. Waldenwood Black Nebula (B-T), Smith

Ch. Westwood Tuf Stuff of Coally (D-S), Lubin & Buchowitz

Am. & Can. Ch. Willow Wand Gold Rush II (D-S), Johnson & Sievert

Ch. Willow Wand Touch O'Talyin (B-S), Hulbert & Runge

Ch. Windhover Sweet Music Man (D-S), Power

Ch. Winsawn's First Choice, UD (D-S), Murphy

Ch. Woodbridge Black Gammon (D-T), Carpenter

Am. & Can. Ch. Wyndcliff Richmore Striking (D-S), Surber

Ch. Younghaven's Grand Slam (D-S), Young (Noted in 1983–84 Handbook as a Gr 1st winner, but not indicated if BIS)

Gaywyn Sandstorm, who, as Birkie, starred in Disney's *The Little Shepherd Dog of Catalina*. Owned by Carol Snip.

Birkie and Bud Parker in the story of the Sheltie that is stranded on Catalina Island, telecast on *The Wonderful World of Disney* in March 1973. © *MCMLXXIII Walt Disney Production world rights reserved.*

28

Birkie, the Shetland Sheepdog Film Star

ON MARCH 11, 1973, Walt Disney Productions released a motion picture on television called *The Little Shepherd Dog of Catalina Island*. The film was one of the Wonderful World of Disney releases, and it was a one-part film produced by Harry Tytle, based on an original script by Rod Peterson. The film was sponsored on TV by Ralston Purina, and millions saw it on a national hookup, either that night or later.

The story features a Shetland Sheepdog, a champion named Birkie, who becomes lost on Catalina Island. He finds his way to a farm where his natural herding abilities are quickly discovered. Bud Parker, the farm's assistant manager, gives him what training he needs.

Eventually, the dog's Mainland California owner discovers his whereabouts. But the dog and Parker are inseparable. And at the moment of coming upon his lost dog, the owner finds Birkie engaged in the dangerous job of rescuing an Arabian stallion who seems likely to fall to his death off a cliff.

Mason decides to leave the Sheltie at Middle Ranch. There, among his normal duties, he stands at stud to bitches sent over to Catalina by his real owner, Mason.

Birkie was a registered Sheltie whose real name was Gaywyn Sandstorm (Shane for short). He was owned by Carol Snip of St. Louis, Missouri. He was a grandson of two Sheltie greats, Ch. Malpsh Great Scot on his sire's side, and Ch. Kawartha's Matchmaker on his dam's side.

The Disney people say they searched for a year before selecting Gaywyn

Sandstorm and Gaywyn Pipedream. Sandstorm had already been given basic obedience training. But let Rod Peterson tell it.

> We brought in the most lovable and understanding Sheltie we had. He walked into Tytle's office confident and self-assured, like any well-trained professional. Tytle stared at the Sheltie for a long moment, and Shane stared right back in eager anticipation. After a few minutes you could see that Harry had taken a liking to him. He issued a couple of simple commands which Shane obeyed perfectly. Then the dog moved up beside Harry's desk and shook hands with him. That sealed the deal. Tytle threw up his hands and said: "Okay, he gets the part!"

Of course, it wasn't quite that simple. Tytle and Peterson wanted two Shelties identical in markings. They had to be of show-dog quality. And they had to be sable color with plain face markings so that they couldn't be confused with the Collie Lassie. The two dogs, Gaywyn Sandstorm and Gaywyn Pipedream, fit those requirements. It was the former who won out and became Birkie in the picture. His training took seven months.

The Collie movie star, Lassie, was not really a lassie but a male dog. Moreover, there were three or four Lassies. They were used for specialized scenes according to their special abilities. If one became ill or otherwise incapacitated, one of the others could take its place. "Lassie" could be making personal appearances at three or four difference places at once.

In *The Little Shepherd Dog of Catalina* there were actually four Shelties. But Gaywyn Sandstorm (the Birkie of the picture) was used in all close-ups, all stills, climbing and running in field scenes, and in some of the tricks that were done. The other three were Piper, Cookie and Banner.

Banner and Cookie were used in some of the herding and chasing scenes. Banner had been trained to attack any animal that the trainers, Clint Rowe and Hubert Wells, ordered it to.

These four dogs, Gaywyn Sandstorm in particular, have done a great deal to inform the American public about Shetland Sheepdogs. To them all, honor!

194

29

Register of Merit
Shelties

M<small>ALES</small> must have sired ten or more champions; bitches must have produced five or more.

Anahassitt April Lady (B)
Anahassitt Atalanta (B)
Ch. Andale A. Sportin' Venture (D)
Annie Laurie of Cross Acres, CD (B)
Ch. Astolat Future Emblem (D)
Ch. Astolat Galaxy, CD (D)
Babinette Mavourneen (B)
Ch. Banchory Back Stop (D)
Ch. Banchory Classic Image (D)
Ch. Banchory Deep Purple (D)
Ch. Banchory Formal Notice (D)
Ch. Banchory High Born (D)
Banchory Mist O'Brigadoon, CD (B)
Banchory Reflection (D)
Ch. Banchory The Cornerstone, CD (D)
Ch. Banchory Thunder Blue (D)
Ch. Barwood Scotchguard Sonata (B)
Ch. Barwoods Bold Venture, CD (D)

Barwoods Formal Attire (D)
Ch. Barwoods Raincheck (D)
Ch. Barwoods Rhapsody (D)
Ch. Barwoods Weather Report (D)
Ch. Benayr Here Comes Trouble (D)
Ch. B'field Crystal Blu Persuasion (B)
Ch. Bil-Bo-Dot Blue Flag of Pocono (D)
Ch. Blue Heritage of Pocono (D)
Ch. Brandell's Break-A-Way II (D)
Ch. Brigadoon Merrilon I'm Ready (D)
Ch. Cahaba's Touch The Wind (D)
Ch. Calcurt Luke (D)
Century Farms Country Charm (B)
Ch. Chenterra Thunderation (D)
Ch. Cherden Sock It To 'Em, CD (D)
China Clipper O'Page's Hill (D)
Ch. Chisterling Falkirks Flame (B)

Ch. Macdega The Piano Man, ROM, owned by Tom Coen, is the sire of over forty American champions.

Ch. Noradel Cimarron, ROM, owned by Loretta Willcuts. *Meneley*

Am., Can. Ch. Banchory Deep Purple, ROM, owned by Dr. and Mrs. Dale B. Gauger, is the sire of thirty champions and a top producer of blue merles.

Am., Can. Ch. Banchory Formal Notice, ROM, was exported to Tetsuo Miyama in Japan by Paul and Donna Tidswell. *Krook*

Ch. Chisterling Falkirk's Flame, ROM, owned by Donald Combee.

Ch. Richmore Repeat Performance, ROM.

January

198

Ch. Chisterling Florian (D)
Ch. Chosen Jubilation, CD (D)
Ch. Creekviews Bit of Honey (B)
Ch. Dan-Dee Portrait In Gold (B)
Ch. Diamond's Robert Bruce (D)
Ch. Dorlane's King Ransome (D)
Ch. Dorlane's Touch of Class, CD (D)
Ch. Elf Dale Viking (D)
Ch. Emphasis Tarocco (B)
Faharaby Blue Babe of Pocono (B)
Fair Play of Sea Isle (D)
Ch. Fourwinds Go For The Gold (B)
Ch. Frigate's Emblem of Astolat (D)
Ch. Geronimo Crown Prince (D)
Ch. Gerthstone's Jon Christopher (D)
Ch. Gra-John's Little Tim Tam (B)
Ch. Halstors Peter Pumpkin (D)
Harvest Hill's Twilite Tear (B)
Ch. Heatherland's Simon Says' (D)
Ch. Ilemist Impossible Dream, CDX (D)
Ch. Karelane Royal Flush O'Kismet (D)
Ch. Karral Good Times (D)
Ch. Kawartha's Fair Game (B)
Kawartha's Match Maker (D)
Ch. Kawartha's Sabrina Fair (B)
Keep Goin' (B)
Ch. Kerianne Sweetqueen (B)
Ch. Kinswood Citation (D)
Ch. Kismet's Conquistador (D)
Ch. Kismet's Dynasty (D)
Kismet's Rubaiyyat (B)
Lady Diana of Rowcliffe (B)
Ch. Larkspur of Pocono, CDX (B)
Ch. Larkspur's Replica of Pocono (B)
Ch. Lingard Centurion O'Cahaba (D)
Ch. Lingard Golden Glow (B)
Ch. Lobo Dell Tangerine O'Dorlane (B)
Lodgewood Sonata (B)
Ch. MacDega Glenhart Grand Prix (D)
Ch. Macdega Mainstay (D)
Ch. Macdega Maserati (D)
Ch. Macdega Proof Positive (D)

Ch. Macdega The Piano Man (D)
Ch. Malpsh Great Scott (D)
Malpsh Her Royal Madjesty (B)
Marisu's Jewel of Arrowhead (B)
Ch. Marwal Steppin' Out (D)
Merri Lon The Blue Tail Fly (D)
Ch. Merry Meddler of Pocono, CDX (D)
Ch. Merrymaker of Pocono, CD (D)
Ch. Midas Citation of Sundial (D)
Ch. Mountaineer O'Page's Hill (D)
Ch. Mowgli (D)
Ch. Musket O'Page's Hill (D)
Ch. Naripa Etudes Lochan Ballad (B)
Ch. Nashcrest Golden Note (D)
Ch. Noradel Cimarron (D)
Ch. Northcountry Westering Son (D)
Ch. Olympic Fairy Flower, CD (B)
Ch. Philidove Heir Presumptive (D)
Ch. Philidove Kismet Jeir Borne (D)
Ch. Pixie Dell Bright Vision (D)
Ch. Prince George O'Page's Hill (D)
Pris (B)
Ch. Richmore Repeat Performance (B)
Ch. Rockwoods Talk To Me (B)
Ch. Romayne's Sportin' Life (D)
Ch. Rorralore-Sportin' Chance, CD (D)
Ch. Sea Isle Serenade (D)
Ch. September The Convincer (D)
Ch. September's Rainmaker (D)
Ch. Shelt-E-Ain Reflection O'Knight (D)
Ch. Sheltieland Shasta Geronimo (B)
Ch. Shu-la-le's Sweet Charity (B)
Ch. Shu-la-le Miss Muffet's Tuffet (B)
Shylove's Rockwood Show-off, CD (B)
Ch. Sir Joshua of Winslow (D)
Ch. Songstress O'Page's Hill (B)
Ch. Stylish Miss of Hatfield (B)
Ch. SumerSong Winter Shadows (D)
Ch. Sundowner Mr. Bojangles, CD (D)
Ch. Sunnybrook's Heritage Spirit (D)

Ch. Diamond's Robert Bruce, ROM, owned by Tentagel Shelties. The painting is by the noted artist and Sheltie fancier Jean Simmonds.

Ch. Cahaba Miss Elegant of Jer Nic, ROM, owned by Ruth G. Mancuso and bred by Ron K. Lackey.

Ch. Thistlerrose Classic Moderne (B) Tull E Ho's Love Token (B)
Timberidge Crown Jewel (B) Ch. Va-Gore's Bright Promise (B)
Ch. Timberidge Temptation (D) Ch. Wayanet's Magic Sandman (D)
Tiny Penny of Walnut Hill, CD (B) Ch. Westwood's Suzy Q (B)
Ch. Tiree Hall Single Image (B) Ch. Willow Wand Touch O'Gold (B)

Listed below are Register of Merit Shetland Sheepdogs that are outstanding for their time in that they will probably influence the breed more in the near future than ROMs or top sires previously listed. Two reasons: sheer numbers, and the fact that they are several times removed from their champion ancestors who were top producers of their day.

ROMs with Twenty or More Champions

Ch. Banchory Back Stop (21) Ch. Macdega Maserati (17)
Ch. Banchory Deep Purple (30) Ch. Macdega Proof Positive (17)
Ch. Banchory Formal Notice (43)* Ch. MacDega The Piano Man (41)
Ch. Banchory High Borne (83) Ch. Malpsh Great Scott (22)
Banchory Reflection (21) Ch. Merrymaker of Pocono, CD (20)
Ch. Chenterra Thunderation (24) Ch. Merry Meddler of Pocono, CDX
Ch. Cherden Sock It to 'Em, CD (31) (20)
Ch. Diamond's Robert Bruce (20) Ch. Mountaineer O'Page's Hill (21)
Ch. Dorlanes King Ransome (20) Ch. Nashcrest Golden Note (24)
Ch. Halstor's Peter Pumpkin (158, all Ch. Romayne's Sportin' Life (50)
time top sire) Ch. Sea Isle Serenade (28)
Ch. Kawartha's Match Maker (22) Ch. September's Rainmaker (21)
Ch. Kismet's Conquistador (31) Ch. Sir John Winslow (20)
Ch. Lingard Sealect Bruce (41, ap- Ch. Sunnybrook's Heritage Spirit (52)
pears in more modern UD pedigrees Ch. Timberidge Temptation (32)
than any other single champion)

Because it's almost impossible for a bitch to produce the numbers of champions that a dog can sire, no bitches have reached the twenty mark. However, there are two who produced more than ten champions.

The all-time top bitch producer is still Ch. Larkspur of Pocono, CDX, with sixteen champions to her credit. She is followed by the nonchampion Kismet's Rubaiyyat with thirteen to her credit. It's also interesting to note that pedigree-wise, both bitches are descended from basically the same genetic family.

Anahassitt Atalanta had an enormous influence on our breed. Almost 80 percent, if not more, of our Shelties were descended from her. The champions listed above, all descended from either Ch. Merrymaker of Pocono, CD/ROM, or Ch. Merry Meddler of Pocono, CDX/ROM, her two sons, are in the background of our modern Shelties.

* title not published

Ch. Halstor's Peter Pumpkin

Ch. Sea Isle Serenade

Ch. Malpsh the Duke of Erle

Sea Isle Dusky Belle

Fair Play of Sea Isle

Ch. Sheltieland Kiltie O'Sea Isle

Ch. Kawartha's Fair Game

Ch. Kawartha's Sabrina Fair

CH. HALSTOR'S PETER PUMPKIN

Ch. Nashcrest Golden Note

Ch. Sea Isle Serenade

Ch. Sea Isle Serenata

Ch. Sea Isle Rhapsody of Halstor

Ch. Sheltieland Kiltie O'Sea Isle

Ch. Colvidale Soliloquy

Ch. Lochelven's Reverie

30

Shetland Sheepdog Pedigrees

HERE WE ARE including the pedigrees of the great dogs of the breed. But more than that, we have selected them on the basis of their bloodlines. We hope, therefore, that most people will be able to trace the background of their dogs through these pedigrees.

Moreover, these pedigrees show, better than any other method, the systems used in developing the breed, for they indicate the ways in which inbreeding, linebreeding and the adding of importations have been used to develop the breed.

Ch. Elf Dale Viking

                    Timberidge Tricolor
             Ch. Noralee Bronze Nugget
                    Timberidge Tessa
      Ch. Noralee Forecaster
                         Ch. Timberidge Temptation
                  Noralee Indian Summer
                         Ch. Noralee Autumn Gold
CH. ELF DALE VIKING
                         Ch. Merrywood's Charter Member
                  Merrywood's Junior Member
                         Merrywood's Will O'The Wisp
      Ch. Elf Dale Heidi
                         Ch. Sea Isle Dappled Grey
                  Ch. Geronimo Little June, CDX
                       Ch. Sheltieland Shasta Geronimo

Ch. Wee Lassie of Eve-Bart, UD

                         Ch. Astolat Golden Symbol
              Park Crest Aladdin
                         Park Crest Princess Hiedi
       Lonnie Du of Eve-Bart
                         Ch. Puck of Perkasie
              Peggy of Fairview
                         Victoria of Perkasie
CH. WEE LASSIE OF EVE-BART, UD
                         Ch. Astolat Golden Symbol
              Park Crest Aladdin
                         Park Crest Princess Hiedi
       Wendy of Eve-Bart
                         Honey Boy of Perkasie
              Honey Girl of Eve-Bart
                         Peggy of Fairview

Am., Can. Ch. Tiree Hall Jedelan Scot

Rosslynn's Replica (Can.)
Ch. Tiree Hall Highland Legend
Ch. Highland Tiree O'Lochindaal
Ch. Tiree Hall Merry Marquis
Rosslynn's Replica (Can.)
Ch. Tiree Hall Single Image
Tiree Hall Kilary Adoration
AM., CAN. CH. TIREE HALL JEDELAN SCOT
Ch. Roc Sycamore Minute Man
Ch. Mori-Brook's "Z" Dancer's Prancer
Teaberry Lane Takes A Notion
Ch. Donamar Candy of Je-Del-An
Ch. Sheltielore Diablo
Al n Phyll Ginger Gumdrop
Chari of Al n Phyll

Ch. Conendale Challenger O'Akirene, CD

Ch. Banchory High Born
Banchory Reflection
Banchory High Glow
Am. & Can. Ch. Banchory Backstop
Banchory Black Gold
Banchory Foxy Lady
Banchory Whipped Cream
CH. CONENDALE CHALLENGER O'AKIRENE, CD
Ch. Banchory The Candidate
Can. Ch. Akirene's Command Performance
Banchory The Black Rose
Akirene's Classic Example
Ch. Banchory The Candidate
Can. Ch. Banchory Coronet
Banchory Love Is Black

Ch. Astolat Galaxy

Ch. Malpsh The Duke of Erle

Fair Play of Sea Isle

Ch. Kawartha's Fair Game

Ch. Halstor's Peter Pumpkin

Ch. Sea Isle Serenade

Ch. Sea Isle Rhapsody of Halstor

Ch. Colvidale Soliloquy

CH. ASTOLAT GALAXY

Ch. Astolat Golden Symbol

Ch. Astolat Gold Award, Int. CD

Scotswold Gretta

Ch. Astolat Stardust

Ch. Gay Piper O'Pages Hill

Ch. Piper's Pride of Astolat

Astolat Symbol's Primrose

J. Ch. Winter Waltz of Katsushika Sanyō

Am. Ch. Halstor's Peter Pumpkin
Am. & Can. Ch. Banchory The Candidate
Banchory High Glow
Can. Ch. Akirene's Commando Performance
Banchory Black Gold
Can. Ch. Banchory The Black Rose, CD
Am. & Can. Ch. Banchory Sugar
J. CH. WINTER WALTZ OF KATSUSHIKA SANYŌ
Am. Ch. Halstor's Peter Pumpkin
Am. & Can. Ch. Banchory The Candidate
Banchory High Glow
Spanish Dance of Katsushika Sanyō
Am. Ch. Wyndliff Ricochet
Joanna of Katsushika Sanyō
Lily of Katsushika Sanyō

209

Am. Ch. Northcountry Westering Son

Am. Ch. Malpsh The Duke of Erle

Fair Play of Sea Isle

Am. Ch. Kawartha's Fair Game

Am. Ch. Halstor's Peter Pumpkin

Am. Ch. Sea Isle Serenade

Am. Ch. Sea Isle Rhapsody of Halstor

Am. Ch. Colvidale Soliloquy

AM. CH. NORTHCOUNTRY WESTERING SON

Fair Play of Sea Isle

Am. Ch. Halstor's Peter Pumpkin

Am. Ch. Sea Isle Rhapsody of Halstor

Am. Ch. Malpsh Count Your Blessings

Am. Ch. Malpsh Great Scott

Malpsh Promises Promises

Pris

ISBN 0-87605-333-9